BUSINESS ISSUES, COMPETITION AND ENTREPRENEURSHIP

PROTECTING WORKERS' RIGHTS WITH U.S. TRADE PARTNERS

FEDERAL EFFORTS

BUSINESS ISSUES, COMPETITION AND ENTREPRENEURSHIP

Additional books in this series can be found on Nova's website under the Series tab.

Additional e-books in this series can be found on Nova's website under the e-book tab.

BUSINESS ISSUES, COMPETITION AND ENTREPRENEURSHIP

PROTECTING WORKERS' RIGHTS WITH U.S. TRADE PARTNERS

FEDERAL EFFORTS

SAMUEL T. STOKES
EDITOR

nova publishers
New York

Library of Congress Cataloging-in-Publication Data

ISBN: 978-1-63483-176-5

Published by Nova Science Publishers, Inc. † New York

CONTENTS

Preface

Protecting workers' rights is a top priority for the Obama Administration, and the Office of the United States Trade Representative (USTR) and the Department of Labor (DOL) are leading the Administration's efforts to improve labor laws and working conditions with trading partners in virtually every region of the globe. These efforts are made in close coordination with other U.S. agencies and in collaboration with Congressional and other stakeholders, as well as international partners such as the International Labour Organization (ILO). This book discusses the Administration's efforts in a number of key countries—Guatemala, Colombia, Jordan, Bahrain, Bangladesh, Swaziland, Haiti and Burma—in which USTR and DOL have had intensive engagement on labor issues in recent years. The book examines steps that selected partner countries have taken, and U.S. assistance they have received, to implement these provisions and other labor initiatives and the reported results of such steps; submissions regarding possible violations of FTA labor provisions that DOL has accepted and any problems related to the submission process; the extent to which U.S. agencies monitor and enforce implementation of FTA labor provisions and report results to Congress.

In: Protecting Workers' Rights ...
Editor: Samuel T. Stokes
ISBN: 978-1-63483-176-5

Chapter 1

STANDING UP FOR WORKERS: PROMOTING LABOR RIGHTS THROUGH TRADE*

Office of the U.S. Trade Representative

EXECUTIVE SUMMARY

Protecting workers' rights is a top priority for the Obama Administration, and the Office of the United States Trade Representative (USTR) and the Department of Labor (DOL) are leading the Administration's efforts to improve labor laws and working conditions with trading partners in virtually every region of the globe. These efforts are made in close coordination with other U.S. agencies and in collaboration with Congressional and other stakeholders, as well as international partners such as the International Labour Organization (ILO).

From bringing the first-ever labor dispute under a free trade agreement (FTA), to working with Burma on a new labor rights initiative, to developing roadmaps to address serious workers' rights concerns in Bangladesh and Swaziland, to seeking the highest-ever labor commitments with the Trans-Pacific Partnership (TPP) and Transatlantic Trade and Investment Partnership (T-TIP) countries, which collectively represent nearly two-thirds of the global economy, the Obama Administration is taking unprecedented actions to

* This is an edited, reformatted and augmented version of a special report issued February 2015.

promote and protect fundamental labor rights and ensure acceptable conditions of work.

The stakes are high and the challenges are great. Overcoming these challenges will require sustained progress across many initiatives and the joining of efforts not only across the U.S. Government but also with other like-minded countries and stakeholders, including the international labor community. With both American values and interests at stake, the Administration is committed to maintaining the effort to ensure that the benefits of trade are broadly shared and to supporting a growing and vibrant middle class around the world.

The trade policy tools that are available to this end have evolved over time. Twenty years ago, when the United States entered into the North American Free Trade Agreement (NAFTA) with Mexico and Canada, labor provisions were not included in the core of the agreement. Rather, they were in a side agreement, virtually all of the provisions of which were not subject to any enforcement mechanism. Today, the Obama Administration is negotiating provisions that are fundamentally different from NAFTA. The Administration is seeking in TPP provisions that require parties to provide workers their fundamental rights, as stated in the ILO Declaration on Fundamental Principles and Rights at Work. The Administration is also seeking first-ever protections relating to importing goods made with forced labor, adopting laws on acceptable conditions of work and upholding labor standards in export processing zones. The Obama Administration has insisted that labor provisions be at the core of the agreement, subject to full dispute settlement and the full range of trade sanctions. Stronger tools make a difference and the new tools being negotiated by the Obama Administration in TPP will empower this Administration—and future administrations—to undertake broader and more effective action than ever before.

This report discusses the Obama Administration's efforts in a number of key countries— Guatemala, Colombia, Jordan, Bahrain, Bangladesh, Swaziland, Haiti and Burma—in which USTR and DOL have had intensive engagement on labor issues in recent years. Presenting unique opportunities and challenges, each country has required a tailored approach—from the invocation of formal dispute settlement procedures, to action under U.S. preference programs, to negotiation of specific commitments for change, to consultations and collaborative efforts to develop a path forward. Our objective, however, has been the same in each case—to make trade work better for workers.

In Guatemala, we are engaged in a formal dispute settlement process under the Dominican Republic-Central America-United States Free Trade Agreement (CAFTA-DR), having exhausted consultative efforts aimed at ensuring that workers are afforded the protections they are due under Guatemalan labor law. As the first Administration to make use of such a mechanism, the Obama Administration has made clear that the objective is not punitive, but rather to ensure that Guatemala upholds the commitments it has made under the CAFTA-DR with respect to workers' rights.

In Bahrain, we have pursued formal consultations under the United States-Bahrain trade agreement to address concerns regarding targeting of union leaders in the events surrounding the 2011 Arab Spring civil unrest. The Government of Bahrain has made important progress—such as reinstating the vast majority of workers who had been dismissed in that process—but significant challenges remain and USTR and DOL are continuing to engage to try to resolve them.

In Colombia, a long and constructive engagement with the Government led to the negotiation of the extensive Colombian Action Plan Related to Labor Rights (Action Plan). This plan was designed to address longstanding concerns relating to violence against labor leaders, impunity for such acts and protection of labor rights. The two countries have worked closely on implementation of the plan, drawing on strong engagement by stakeholders in both countries. Important progress has been made but much more work remains and the United States will continue to work closely with Colombia in this process.

In Jordan, our engagement produced an Implementation Plan Related to Working and Living Conditions of Workers that is helping to address concerns about workers' rights and working conditions in Jordan's garment sector, particularly with respect to foreign workers. Jordan has issued new standards for dormitory inspections, submitted new labor legislation to its parliament and hired new labor inspectors. The ILO has also been an important partner and has ramped up its engagement in Jordan to support labor protections for foreign workers.

Bangladesh, Swaziland, & Haiti illustrate how the Administration has been using the tools in U.S. preference programs to protect labor rights. Each of these countries is eligible for benefits under different programs—Bangladesh from the Generalized System of Preferences (GSP), Swaziland from the African Growth and Opportunity Act (AGOA) and Haiti from the Hemispheric Opportunity through Partnership Encouragement (HOPE) program. These programs, which encourage economic growth in developing countries through trade, all condition preferential market access on meeting certain "eligibility criteria," which include criteria relating to labor rights. While the specific labor criteria in each program are unique, the Obama Administration has made use of all of them to address a range of serious problems: from lack of worker voice, to building and fire safety concerns, to acts of violence and intimidation towards union organizers, to employment-related sexual harassment. Addressing these issues is not only critical to protecting workers' rights, it is necessary for strengthening developing countries' growth strategies.

In Burma, we are developing new tools suited to the particular economic conditions in that country. We have announced a joint *Initiative to Promote Fundamental Labor Rights and Practices in Myanmar*, which aims to establish a partnership to advance labor rights and protections for workers in Burma. With recent changes in its posture towards the outside world, Burma is at an early and pivotal stage in its economic growth. The Initiative helps Burma lay the right foundation for ensuring that economic growth and development proceed on a basis that is inclusive and sustainable.

Finally, this report discusses the labor rights commitments that the United States is negotiating as part of the landmark *Trans-Pacific Partnership (TPP)* agreement with 11 Asia-Pacific countries and the *Transatlantic Trade and Investment Partnership (T-TIP)* agreement with the 28 European Union member states. These agreements present an opportunity to lock in and build on the progress that we have made in ensuring that protection of labor rights is a core component of U.S. trade policy and helping to create new global norms for protecting workers' rights in the context of trade.

TIMELINE

Key Obama Administration Engagement

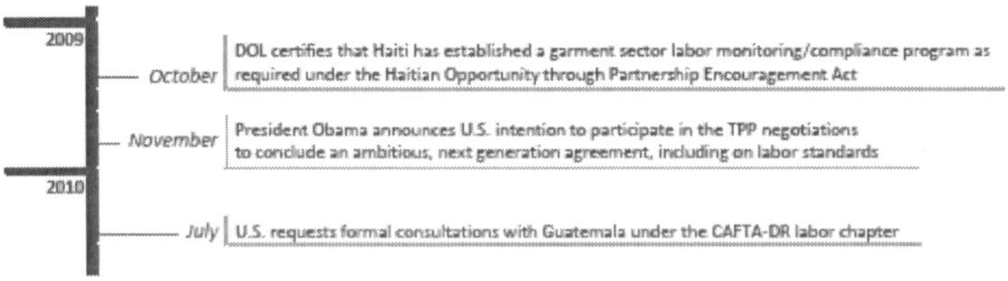

2011

- *April* — U.S. and Colombia sign the Labor Action Plan
- *June* — DOL accept a labor submission under the U.S-Bahrain free trade agreement
- *August* — U.S. requests first-ever establishment of an arbitral panel against Guatemala under the CAFTA-DR labor chapter

2012

- *December* — DOL issues the Bahrain labor report, responding to concerns regarding targeting of union leaders in the events surrounding the 2011 Arab Spring civil unrest

2013

- *January* — U.S. and Jordan sign an Implementation Plan Related to Working & Living Conditions of Workers to address concerns about worker rights and conditions in Jordan's garment sector
- *April* — U.S. and Guatemala sign an 18-point Enforcement Plan to address concerns in the labor submission and panel process is suspended to afford Guatemala time to implement
- *May* — U.S. requests formal consultations with Bahrain under the labor chapter of the Bahrain FTA
- *June* — - U.S. suspends Bangladesh's eligibility under the Generalized System of Preferences program because of failure to meet the labor eligibility criteria
  - U.S. and EU announce the launch of negotiations on the Transatlantic Trade and Investment Partnership, including high-standard labor provisions
- *July* — U.S. joins the EU, the ILO, and the Government of Bangladesh under the "Sustainability Compact" on worker rights and factory safety in the garment sector in Bangladesh
- *December* — DOL and the Jordanian Ministry of Labour sign a MOU establishing a labor cooperation mechanism that includes funding a garment-sector monitoring and enforcement program run by the ILO (Better Work Jordan)

2014

- *June* — President Obama announces withdrawal of Swaziland's eligibility under the African Growth and Opportunity Act, effective January 2015, for failure to meet labor eligibility criteria
- *September* — U.S. resumes panel arbitration process against Guatemala under labor chapter of CAFTA-DR because of failure to fully implement Enforcement Plan
- *November* — U.S., Burma, Japan, Denmark and the ILO formally launch the Initiative to Promote Fundamental Labor Rights and Practices in Myanmar.

GUATEMALA

KEY EXPORTS TO THE UNITED STATES:

Bananas & plantains, unroasted coffee, fresh fruit, processed fruit and vegetables

LABOR FORCE:

6,036,000 workers

RELEVANT TRADE POLICY TOOLS:

Dominican Republic-Central America-United States Free Trade Agreement and 2013 Enforcement Plan

Overview

Guatemala and the United States are both parties to the Dominican Republic-Central America-United States Free Trade Agreement (CAFTA-DR). That agreement—which was signed in 2004 and also includes the Dominican Republic, El Salvador, Costa Rica, Honduras, and Nicaragua—requires that parties effectively enforce their labor laws. If a country does not comply with that obligation, it can be taken before a dispute settlement panel. And if the panel finds against the country, it can be subjected to an annual "monetary assessment" (i.e., a fine) until that country comes into compliance.

On August 9, 2011, the United States requested the establishment of a dispute settlement panel, asserting that Guatemala was not effectively enforcing labor laws relating to the right of association, the right to organize and bargain collectively, and acceptable conditions of work. In so doing, the Obama Administration became the first in history to bring a labor case under a free trade agreement—not just under a U.S. trade agreement, but any trade agreement ever negotiated.

The Guatemala case was initiated pursuant to a submission by the AFL-CIO and six Guatemalan labor organizations to the U.S. Government under the CAFTA-DR labor chapter. The submission outlined concerns, including regarding Guatemala's enforcement of its labor laws in key sectors—apparel, bananas, processed fruits and vegetables and ports—and argued that these cases illustrated a broader failure to enforce labor laws.

USTR and DOL worked closely with the submitters and with the Government of Guatemala to evaluate the allegations, both the specific cases identified as well as the broader enforcement concerns raised. As a result, USTR and DOL identified a number of apparent failures to enforce Guatemalan labor law including:

1. Failure by the Guatemalan Ministry of Labor to investigate alleged labor law violations;
2. Failure by the Guatemalan Ministry of Labor to take enforcement action once it identifies a labor law violation; and
3. Failure to enforce labor court orders in cases involving labor law violations.

At the same time that they investigated the allegations, USTR and DOL engaged the Government of Guatemala with the aim of resolving the concerns as quickly and effectively as possible.

Bilateral engagement is often the quickest path to resolution of concerns under trade agreements and is the first resort in all cases, whether they involve labor or other trade agreement obligations. In Guatemala's case, however, bilateral engagement failed to resolve the issues and in July 2010, USTR and DOL requested consultations under the CAFTA-DR labor chapter. When labor consultations did not result in a resolution, USTR initiated formal dispute settlement steps —first, with a meeting of the Free Trade Commission and, when that did not resolve the issues, with a request that a CAFTA-DR dispute settlement panel be established to review the case.

In an attempt to resolve the dispute, the U.S. Government agreed to suspend the panel process while it worked with the Guatemalan Government to establish a plan identifying significant, concrete steps that the Guatemalan Government could take, within specific timeframes, to improve enforcement of labor laws. Signed by the two governments on April 25, 2013, the 18-point Enforcement Plan included actions to address key concerns in the labor submission and in the subsequent analyses by USTR and DOL. To facilitate Guatemala's implementation of the plan, USTR agreed to continue the panel suspension.

USTR and DOL engaged extensively with Guatemalan officials to support implementation of the Enforcement Plan, including through several trips to Guatemala to meet directly with the Government and Guatemalan workers. Engagement occurred at the highest levels, with U.S. Trade Representative Froman meeting with President Perez Molina of Guatemala on July 25, 2014, in Washington, DC, to urge Guatemala to complete the steps laid out in the Enforcement Plan.

On July 31, 2014, at the request of the Guatemalan President, Ambassador Froman travelled to Guatemala to deliver the same message to a wide range of stakeholders, which included Guatemalan congressional leaders from across the political spectrum, the Ministers of Labor, Economy, and Foreign Affairs and Guatemalan labor and business groups.

Ambassador Froman also met with the International Labor Organization and the United Nations to discuss coordination of efforts in pushing Guatemala to implement needed changes.

Progress

Since the signing of the Enforcement Plan in April 2013, Guatemala has taken important steps to implement the Enforcement Plan. To enhance the Ministry of Labor's enforcement of labor laws, Guatemala:

- Hired 100 new inspectors.
- Issued a number of legal instruments to ensure police assistance to facilitate labor inspector access to worksites.

To strengthen the enforcement of labor court orders, Guatemala:

- Created a new "Verification Unit" within the judiciary with standardized procedures and criteria for verifying employer compliance with labor court orders.
- Conducted a review of labor courts in an effort to hold accountable judges who fail to take the measures required by law to enforce court orders.

To better incentivize export companies to comply with labor laws, Guatemala published Ministerial Accords that:

- Establish a public comment process as part of the review of applications by export companies for certain tax benefits and require rejection of applications from companies that are found to have violated labor laws.
- stablish a streamlined process to revoke the tax benefits for existing beneficiaries that violate labor laws and publish the names of companies whose benefits are withdrawn.
- equire the Ministry of Labor to conduct annual inspections of all enterprises receiving the special tax benefits.

To address the closure of enterprises without payment to workers of salaries and other benefits due under Guatemalan labor laws, Guatemala:

- *Issued Ministerial Accords requiring the intervention of the Labor Ministry* when it receives information of a potential enterprise closure and directing the Ministry to take the steps necessary to secure payment to workers if the enterprise closes, including by petitioning relevant labor courts to embargo or seize assets.

Remaining Challenges

Critical Enforcement Plan commitments by the Guatemalan Government remain outstanding. These include, for example:

- Enacting legislation to expedite the sanctioning of employers that violate labor laws.
- Issuing and publicizing standardized timeframes for labor inspections and criteria for determining when "employer substitution" has occurred (e.g., where a company purports to go out of business but re-establishes under a different name).
- Demonstrating that the reforms that Guatemala has adopted have been implemented and that they are leading to sufficient concrete improvements with respect to workers' rights and working conditions on the ground.

As a result, on September 18, 2014, the Obama Administration decided to lift the suspension of the panel process and proceed with the case against Guatemala. An outcome in the Guatemala case is expected in 2015.

Looking Ahead

Even as the dispute process moves ahead, the United States will continue to press Guatemala to undertake the efforts needed to come into compliance with its obligations under the CAFTA-DR. Our hope remains that there can be continued progress and the outstanding concerns in the case can be resolved collaboratively and expeditiously.

Bahrain

KEY EXPORTS TO THE UNITED STATES:
Aluminum, woven apparel, mineral oil, fertilizers

LABOR FORCE:
741,700 workers

RELEVANT TRADE POLICY TOOLS:
U.S.-Bahrain Free Trade Agreement

Overview

The United States and Bahrain entered into a free trade agreement on September 14, 2004. On labor, the agreement committed the two parties to enforce their own labor laws and to strive to ensure that internationally recognized labor rights are recognized and protected by their laws. These provisions could be the subject of formal consultations under the agreement, but only the provision regarding enforcement of labor laws could be the subject of dispute settlement.

In April 2011, DOL received a submission from the AFL-CIO on behalf of the General Federation of Bahrain Trade Unions. The submission alleged that Bahrain's actions against trade unionists in response to civil unrest and national strikes in early 2011 violated the unionists' rights to freedom of association and nondiscrimination in employment. According to the submission, these actions violated Bahrain's commitments under the labor chapter of the free trade agreement.

On June 10, 2011, DOL accepted the AFL-CIO submission for review. As part of its review, DOL considered detailed and voluminous information received from the Government of Bahrain and Bahraini workers, amendments to the Bahraini Trade Union Law, and labor-related developments in international fora regarding Bahrain, in particular at the ILO. In addition, two DOL delegations visited Bahrain in October 2011 and February 2012 for fact-finding, as well as consultations with the Government of Bahrain.

In December 2012, after completing its review, DOL issued a public report finding that trade unionists were targeted for dismissal, and in some cases prosecuted, for their role in organizing and participating in the March 2011 general strike. The report also found that Shia workers and political critics of the Bahraini administration faced discimination. In addition, the report raised concerns about violations of freedom of association and political and religious (sectarian) discrimination against Shia workers in the reinstatement process. The report made specific recommendations for the Government of Bahrain to address the issues identified and to facilitate compliance with commitments under the labor chapter.

On May 6, 2013, the United States formally requested labor consultations with Bahrain under the labor chapter of the trade agreement. Beginning in July 2013, the United States held two rounds of consultations with Bahrain in an effort to develop initiatives to address identified concerns about employment discrimination and freedom of association.

Progress

Over the course of USTR and DOL's engagement, the Government of Bahrain made progress in the following areas:

- Reinstatement of dismissed workers. The Government of Bahrain worked with private businesses, state-owned companies and workers' organizations to re-instate more than 95 percent of workers who were dismissed during the period of civil unrest in early 2011.
- Tripartite agreement to address issues of concern. The Government of Bahrain signed an agreement in 2014 with workers' and employers' organizations to address many of the issues, including employment discrimination, stemming from the 2011 dismissals. This agreement led to the successful closing of a complaint filed by Bahrain's unions with the ILO.
- Labor reforms. In 2014, the Government of Bahrain submitted labor reforms to Bahrain's parliament to remove restrictions on multiple-sector labor federations and to clarify the process for selecting worker representatives in international bodies and national-level collective bargaining.

Remaining Challenges

USTR and DOL are continuing with the process of consultations to encourage and assist the Government of Bahrain to make progress on the remaining challenges, including:

- Compliance with labor laws related to anti-union harassment and intimidation, union dues deduction and collective bargaining, particularly in the context of recent reforms that allow for multiple unions in the workplace.
- Review and amendment of Bahraini labor law in furtherance of the commitment to strive to ensure that international labor standards with respect to freedom of association and employment discrimination are recognized and protected, including by:
    - Repealing bans on public sector unions, multi-sector labor federations, political activity by unions, and a wide range of strikes, significant restrictions on union leadership and criminal sanctions for strikes in public services;
    - Banning employment discrimination, including based on political opinion and religion.
- Development of new procedures and guidelines for the receipt and adjudication of allegations of discrimination in the workplace and for redress and sanctions for violations identified.
- Strengthening of tripartite social dialogue through regular meetings and discussion of impediments to observance of international labor standards in the context of industrial relations and employment discrimination.

Looking Ahead

USTR and DOL, together with the State Department, are continuing to support the Government of Bahrain's efforts to address remaining concerns regarding freedom of association and employment discrimination related to the civil protests in 2011. The aim is to help Bahrain return to its previous status among the leaders in the Gulf on labor matters.

Colombia

KEY EXPORTS TO THE UNITED STATES:
Crude oil, gold, spices, coffee, cut flowers, bananas

LABOR FORCE:
23,107,300 workers

RELEVANT TRADE/LABOR POLICY TOOLS:
U.S.-Colombia Trade Promotion Agreement and Colombian Action Plan Related to Labor Rights

Overview

Through the United States-Colombia Trade Promotion Agreement (TPA), the Obama Administration has sought to address some of the longest-standing and most intractable concerns about labor rights and working conditions of any trading partners. In 2006, when the Bush Administration concluded the Colombia TPA , the State Department's Human Rights Report identified a range of labor concerns in Colombia, including violence and discrimination against trade union members to discourage workers from joining unions and engaging in union activity; impunity for acts of labor-related violence; a proliferation of fake worker "cooperatives" that were used to undermine workers' rights; and use of "collective pacts" with favorable terms negotiated directly with individual workers to weaken existing unions and avoid collective bargaining.

At that time, many in Congress were also demanding that all pending free trade agreements, including the Colombia TPA, be renegotiated to include strong labor protections, including an enforceable commitment to adopt and maintain fundamental rights as stated in the ILO *Declaration on Fundamental Principles and Rights at Work.* A bipartisan agreement between the Congress and the Administration, known as the "May 10, 2007, agreement," reflected these concerns.

In June 2007, the Colombia TPA was renegotiated to include elements of this bipartisan "May 10" agreement. However, it was not until after the Obama Administration came into office in 2009 that efforts were made to address the specific concerns raised in the Colombian context and to develop a roadmap for moving forward.

Labor Action Plan

Working closely with Congressional and other stakeholders, the U.S. Government negotiated with the Colombian Government a detailed "Colombian Action Plan Related to Labor Rights" (Action Plan). The Action Plan specified concrete steps that Colombia would take to address the major areas of concern, including with respect to violence against unionists, impunity for the perpetrators of the violence and protection of labor rights. The two governments initialed the Action Plan on April 7, 2011.

The United States has worked with Colombia on implementation of the Action Plan, including supporting the establishment of a separate Ministry of Labor to elevate the importance of labor issues within the Colombian Government. Regular meetings and ongoing engagement between the U.S. and Colombian Governments have also focused on achieving the underlying goals of the Action Plan, including through technical assistance and cooperation activities to help build the institutional capacity of Colombia's Ministry of Labor.

Today, Colombia presents a record of both meaningful progress in areas of key importance under the Action Plan, as well as areas of concern that will require additional effort to address.

Working to End Violence & Impunity

The Action Plan took a two-pronged approach to addressing the long-standing concerns about violence against unionists and labor activists and impunity for the perpetrators:

1. It called upon Colombia to strengthen and make more accessible protections offered by Colombia's National Protection Unit (UNP), a unit housed within Colombia's Ministry of Interior that protects individuals, groups and communities facing an extraordinary or extreme risk of targeted violence.
2. It committed Colombia to more effectively prosecute perpetrators of violence against trade unionists and labor activists.

Progress

Colombia has made progress in a number of areas:

- Improving confidence in the protection program. 677 union members are currently in the protection program. 248 vehicles and 609 bodyguards are assigned to union leaders and labor activists for full-time protection. To date, no unionist under the protection program has been killed.
- Additional prosecutors and police investigators. In 2011, Colombia's Prosecutor General assigned over 20 prosecutors exclusively to crimes against union members and labor activists and Colombia's National Police assigned an additional 100 full-time judicial police investigators to support the prosecutors. Currently, 23 prosecutors across the country comprise the specialized sub-unit of the Prosecutor General's Office that focuses on violence against unionists and labor activists. Approximately 80 judicial police investigators support the work of the prosecutors.
- Conviction of Intellectual authors. In two landmark cases in 2013, Colombian courts convicted the "intellectual authors" of the 2001 murders of two union leaders in the coal sector and one in the agriculture sector and sentenced the perpetrators to 38 years and 17 years in prison, respectively. Stakeholders have long pressed the Colombian authorities to investigate and bring to justice such "intellectual authors" and not just the trigger men who directly commit the crimes.
- A steady decline in Colombian homicide rates, including for union members and labor activists. This trend continued in the period since the Action Plan was announced. From 2001 to 2010, Colombian experts reported an average of close to 100 murders per year of union members. From 2011 to 2014, the number dropped to an average of 28. The United States is committed to working with Colombia to ensure that this trend continues until there are no more labor-motivated murders and union members no longer fear for their lives.

Remaining Challenges

- The slow pace of prosecutions and convictions in recent labor homicides. According to the Prosecutor General's Office, in the 110 labor homicides that have occurred since 2011, there have been only four convictions. The Prosecutor General reports having arrested 28 suspects in an additional 16 cases.
- An increase in threats against labor leaders and activists, particularly through text messages, phone calls, letters, emails and other forms of communication that are often difficult to trace. The Prosecutor General has assigned prosecutors and investigators to cases of threats against labor leaders and activists. However, to date, no threat case, of the over 1,100 reported by the Government since 2011, has been successfully resolved.
- Concerns that bodyguards hired through private contractors may not undergo adequate background checks and may be more susceptible to corruption. The Colombian Government is transitioning to direct hiring of all bodyguards who provide protection.

More progress is needed to lower the incidence of threats and violence, and the U.S. Government is engaged with the Government of Colombia and international partners, like the ILO, to provide critical assistance. For example, the U.S. Agency for International Development (USAID) is providing roughly $125,000 per year to the UNP. In addition, DOL has been funding a five-year, $7.8 million ILO project the includes a focus on building the institutional capacity of the Colombian Government to combat impunity for perpetrators of violence against trade union leaders, members and activists, including through training of Colombian prosecutors, investigators and judges on labor rights and on investigating such crimes.

Strengthening Labor Laws & Enforcement

Progress

Colombia has also taken important steps to strengthen labor laws and their enforcement.

- Ban on abuse of cooperatives and other similar employment relationships. The Colombian Government enacted new legal provisions and regulations in 2011 and 2013 to prohibit and sanction with significant fines, the misuse of cooperatives and other employment relationships that undermine workers' rights. A recent ruling by the Colombian Constitutional Court strengthens inspectors' ability to investigate these relationships.
- Increase in labor inspectors. Starting in June 2011, the Ministry of Labor has increased the size of the labor inspectorate from 424 inspectors to 718 inspectors, with an additional 188 slated to be hired.
- *Inspections conducted in priority* sectors. Since January 2014, labor inspectors have undertaken 54 investigations in the five priority sectors of palm oil, sugar, mines, ports and flowers for illegal subcontracting.
- *Fines imposed for unlawful subcontracting*. The Ministry of Labor has levied $31 million in fines for unlawful subcontracting that undermines workers' rights (e.g., unlawful cooperatives), from 2011 to date. In 2013, the agency charged with collecting fines for labor violations announced new rules to improve its fine collection ability, in particular authorizing the agency to require and hold collateral payment from an enterprise pending the outcome of a judicial appeal of a fine.
- *Decline of cooperatives in sugar sector.* As of April 2014, more than 70 percent of sugar cane cutters (totaling roughly 7,000 workers) who were previously in unlawful cooperatives have formed unions and negotiated collective bargaining agreements with subsidiaries of the main sugar processing companies. Although the workers are employees of the subsidiaries and not the main companies themselves, labor unions in the sugar sector report that the subsidiaries are properly funded and that the unions are able to negotiate over wages and working conditions with them.
- *Reform of criminal code.* In 2011, as specified in the Action Plan, the Colombian Congress reformed the criminal code, establishing criminal penalties and possible imprisonment for employers that undermine the right to organize and bargain collectively, including by extending better conditions to non-union workers through collective pacts. It will be important to see whether any investigations under these reforms lead to convictions and, where warranted, successful

"conciliations" (Government-led efforts to resolve alleged violations through voluntary negotiations between workers and employers).

Remaining Challenges

There are also areas where further work is needed to strengthen Colombia's labor law regime and practices, including the following:

- Limited fine collection. The Colombian authorities have only collected roughly five percent of the $31 million in fines levied for illegal subcontracting since 2011, according to the most recent information from the Colombian Government.
- Increased abuse of other forms of indirect employment. The number of unlawful cooperatives has dropped significantly, largely in response to Colombia's focus on strengthening and applying labor laws intended to combat such arrangements. However, many employers have shifted to other forms of unlawful subcontracting that similarly avoid direct employment relationships and undermine workers' rights, such as simplified stock companies (known as SASs). The Colombian Government is developing tools to address this problem, including a new legal instrument explicitly targeting such alternative forms of unlawful subcontracting.
- Implementation of certain "formalization agreements" that undermine workers' rights. Colombia has established a mechanism—known as "formalization agreements"—to hire workers previously in unlawful subcontracting relationships, in part to bolster the Action Plan goals of shifting those workers into long-term direct employment relationships. While the development of the "formalization agreement" mechanism is positive, there have been concerns about implementation in some cases. That includes, for example, negotiation of agreements that do not require direct employment relationships or permanent contracts with the main enterprise benefiting from the labor and agreements that do not cover all workers affected by illegal subcontracting.

To help Colombia meet the labor law and enforcement challenges that still exist, DOL is funding a five-year, $7.8 million ILO project that is focused on strengthening the overall capacity of the Colombian Ministry of Labor. DOL is also funding a three-year, $1.5 million project started in 2012 with Colombia's National Union School (Escuela Nacional Sindical), a labor rights NGO, to create "Workers' Rights Centers" in four Colombian cities. The centers provide free legal advice to workers to raise awareness of labor laws and improve workers' ability to protect and claim their labor rights, for example, by filing well-documented complaints with the Ministry of Labor.

Looking Ahead

Most of the issues that are the subject of the Action Plan have a long history in Colombia and addressing them will require continued engagement. Towards that end, U.S. Trade Representative Froman met with Colombian Minister of Commerce Industry and Tourism, Santiago Rojas Arroyo, on April 4, 2014, to urge additional actions in areas where concerns remain. On October 21, 2014, Secretary of Labor Perez met with Colombian Minister of Labor Luis Eduardo "Lucho" Garzón to discuss remaining challenges such as collecting fines in cases of unlawful subcontracting, effectively targeting shifting forms of unlawful subcontracting and investigating and prosecuting the most recent cases of violence against trade unionists. Further engagement is also being discussed for 2015 and beyond.

USTR and DOL are committed to continuing to work in close collaboration with stakeholders in both countries and with the Colombian Government to achieve the underlying goals of the Action Plan and to support the efforts of workers to exercise their fundamental rights.

JORDAN

KEY EXPORTS TO THE UNITED STATES:
Knit and woven apparel, jewelry, miscellaneous textile articles, pharmaceutical products

LABOR FORCE:
1,898,000 workers

RELEVANT TRADE POLICY TOOLS:
U.S.-Jordan Free Trade Agreement, Implementation Plan Related to Working and Living Conditions of Workers, and Memorandum of Understanding Establishing a Labor Cooperation Mechanism

Overview

The United States and Jordan entered into a free trade agreement on October 24, 2000. The agreement commits both parties to enforce their labor laws and to strive to ensure that internationally recognized labor rights are recognized and protected by domestic law. The agreement was viewed by many as a significant step forward in U.S. trade and labor policy because, for the first time, the labor obligations were included in the core text, not a side agreement as in the earlier NAFTA. They were also made subject to the same dispute settlement processes available for the other parts of the agreement.

USTR and DOL have cited these provisions of the U.S.-Jordan FTA in their efforts to address significant concerns that have been raised with respect to worker rights and working conditions in Jordan's garment sector, especially with respect to foreign workers.

The 2012 State Department Human Rights Report on Jordan noted, for example, that "NGOs reported that foreign migrant workers, including garment workers and domestic workers, were especially vulnerable to sexual harassment, including sexual assault, in the workplace."

The report also noted that, although foreign workers were allowed to join unions, "[o]bservers reported it was common practice for management to refuse to renew foreign workers' contracts on the basis of 'troublemaking' or attempting to organize in the workplace." Further, the report noted that "[i]n the garment sector foreign workers were more susceptible than their Jordanian counterparts to dangerous or unfair conditions, including mandatory overtime, delayed payment of wages, deductions for room and board, and unacceptable dormitory conditions."

Beginning in 2011 the U.S. Government engaged in consultations with stakeholders and the Government of Jordan to understand these concerns and to negotiate a resolution. As a result of this engagement, in January 2013, the United States and Jordan agreed to an Implementation Plan Related to Working and Living Conditions of Workers to address anti-union and gender discrimination against foreign workers, including sexual harassment and improve foreign workers' dormitory accommodations.

In addition, DOL signed a Memorandum of Understanding with the Jordanian Ministry of Labor in December 2013 to develop a labor cooperation mechanism. As part of this cooperation, DOL is funding the ILO Better Work Jordan program that monitors and reports publicly on workers' rights and working conditions in more than 90 percent of Jordan's garment factories.

Progress

Through these and other efforts there has been important progress in a number of areas.

- New dormitory inspection processes and "accommodation criteria." Jordan has issued new protocols and procedures for inspecting dormitories at garment factories, as well as new "accommodation criteria," which include requirements for sleeping quarters, bathrooms and general health and safety measures. The United States is working with Jordan to help ensure the Jordanian Ministries of Health and Labor closely cooperate on inspections to enforce the new standards and address violations.
- Formation of an independent worker federation. In April 2013, the first independent worker federation in Jordan, the Federation of Independent Trade Unions of Jordan, was established. The Federation

represents nine Jordanian trade unions, which in turn represent more than 7,000 workers. The Solidarity Center, which has supported the efforts of Jordanian workers to organize, hailed the development saying it "demonstrate[d] a concrete commitment to independent trade unionism as workers in Jordan seek to mobilize for greater political freedom, improved economic conditions and strong social justice."

Under the Better Work Jordan program, the ILO has constructed and opened a state-of-the-art workers' center in Jordan's largest export processing zone, the Al-Hassan Industrial Zone. The workers' center is a 1,300 square meter facility with indoor recreational and learning space that provides workers with access to exercise facilities; legal advice, including on issues of as sexual harassment and union representation; and mental health and counseling services. Facilities include a computer lab with 30 computers and a canteen, and services offered include job skills training and cultural orientation for newly-arrived migrant workers. The workers' center is also supported by USAID, the Al-Hassan Industrial Zone Authority, apparel factories at the Al-Hassan Industrial Zone, the garment workers' union, and international clothing brands. The Center also provides an ILO training program on promoting gender equality in the workplace, which has already trained close to one hundred women workers.

- Signing of a landmark collective bargaining agreement. In May 2013, the Jordanian Garment Workers' Union and Jordan's garment industry signed a landmark collective bargaining agreement which is one of the most comprehensive in the garment sector globally. The agreement contains provisions on dormitory standards, annual seniority bonuses, dispute settlement, trade union recognition and employer rights.
- New labor legislation developed. In 2014, Jordan submitted new labor legislation to its parliament in the areas of collective bargaining, trade union rights, and employment.

USTR and DOL have continued intensive work to follow up on implementation of the commitments under the Implementation Plan. In June 2014, the agencies conducted a monitoring trip to Jordan which included site visits to several garment factories and worker dormitories.

During the same month, USTR and DOL convened a meeting of the FTA Labor Subcommittee in Amman, Jordan, to engage directly with

Jordanian senior officials from the Ministry of Labor on the Implementation Plan. The Labor Subcommittee held in-depth discussions on several topics related to FTA labor commitments including strengthening the Ministry of Labor's labor law enforcement capacity; combatting gender discrimination, including sexual harassment; improving occupational safety and health; and strengthening social dialogue between the government, employers and workers.

Remaining Challenges

Challenges remain with respect to Jordan's implementation of commitments to address labor concerns, including:

- Issuing and applying directives clarifying garment sector workers' rights in connection to anti-union and gender discrimination, including related sexual harassment, and to union representatives' access to workers.
- Developing and implementing procedures for joint Ministries of Health and Labor inspections of dormitories in the garment sector to ensure compliance with new dormitory standards.
- Ensuring that union representatives have access to workers, without fear of reprisals and that the landmark garment sector collective bargaining agreement is applied equally to all workers, including migrants.
- Ensuring effective outreach to migrant workers on gender and anti-union discrimination, including by increasing the availability and foreign language capacity of Ministry of Labor inspectors and hotlines.
- Training and equipping police to effectively protect the safety of female workers, in particular in police stations near and in industrial zones.

Looking Ahead

USTR and DOL, together with the U.S. Embassy in Amman, are continuing to work closely with the Government of Jordan on labor matters, in particular to ensure ongoing progress under the Implementation Plan, and to cooperate under the Memorandum of Understanding.

The U.S. Government will continue to systemically monitor and work to address the remaining challenges to fulfillment of the Implementation Plan commitments and application of the garment sector collective bargaining agreement, including in the course of the cooperative labor dialogue under the FTA. DOL has also committed an additional $1 million to support Better Work Jordan's efforts to help ensure that garment factories comply with internationally-recognized labor standards.

The U.S. and Jordanian Governments will also continue to cooperate to improve labor law enforcement nationally. For example, at the request of the Jordanian Government, DOL has provided a $2 million extension for an ILO project to facilitate implementation of Jordan's National Framework on Child Labor, including by improving enforcement of child labor laws, raising awareness of child labor, and referring at-risk children and families to social services and educational and vocational opportunities.

BANGLADESH

KEY EXPORTS TO THE UNITED STATES:
Apparel, textiles, headgear, shrimp and prawns, agricultural products (primarily tobacco)

LABOR FORCE:
78,820,000 workers

RELEVANT TRADE POLICY TOOLS:
Generalized System of Preferences and EU-US-ILO-Bangladesh Sustainability Compact

Overview

Bangladesh does not have a trade agreement with the United States; rather it is a beneficiary of a U.S. trade "preference program" known as the Generalized System of Preferences (GSP). That program, designed to promote economic growth and sustainable development in the developing world, provides duty-free access to the U.S. market for approximately 5,000 products from 122 beneficiary countries, provided that the countries meet certain eligibility criteria. On labor, the GSP program requires that beneficiary countries be "taking steps to afford internationally recognized worker rights." Under the GSP statute, failure to meet the eligibility criteria is grounds for suspending benefits under the program. For the Obama Administration, the GSP labor eligibility review process has provided an important avenue to address serious labor concerns in developing countries, including Bangladesh.

The expansion of the garment industry has revolutionized the economy of Bangladesh. It has grown GDP and provided opportunities for millions of workers and their families. But the industry's rapid growth has also presented enormous challenges for the Government of Bangladesh and for the industry itself, including for ensuring compliance with basic workplace safety laws and fundamental labor rights.

The combination of extraordinary business growth and inadequate worker protections has had tragic consequences. By 2012, there were frequent reports of fatal factory fires, unpaid wages, assaults on labor leaders and large-scale worker demonstrations. In November 2012, a fire at the Tazreen Fashions garment factory killed 117 workers, many of whom worked behind gated windows and locked exits.

Several months later, in April 2013, the multi-story Rana Plaza building, which housed several garment factories, collapsed, killing 1,129 men and women. Although serious structural cracks had been discovered in the building before the collapse, factory managers insisted that workers continue working in the building under threat of termination.

For a number of years before these two tragedies, the U.S. Government had been pressing the Bangladeshi Government, as part of an ongoing "eligibility review" under the GSP program, to make significant improvements in its workers' rights and worker safety laws and practices. Despite some early encouraging signs that the Government of Bangladesh was addressing the underlying issues, by late 2012 the situation had deteriorated and reports of workers' rights violations and safety concerns had escalated.

In January 2013, USTR announced that, in view of the lack of progress by the Government of Bangladesh in addressing workers' rights and worker safety issues, it was considering a recommendation to the President to withdraw or suspend Bangladesh's trade benefits under GSP. The Rana Plaza tragedy, three months later, underscored the seriousness of the concerns. On

June 27, 2013, following an extensive interagency review, President Obama announced his decision to suspend Bangladesh's trade benefits under GSP.

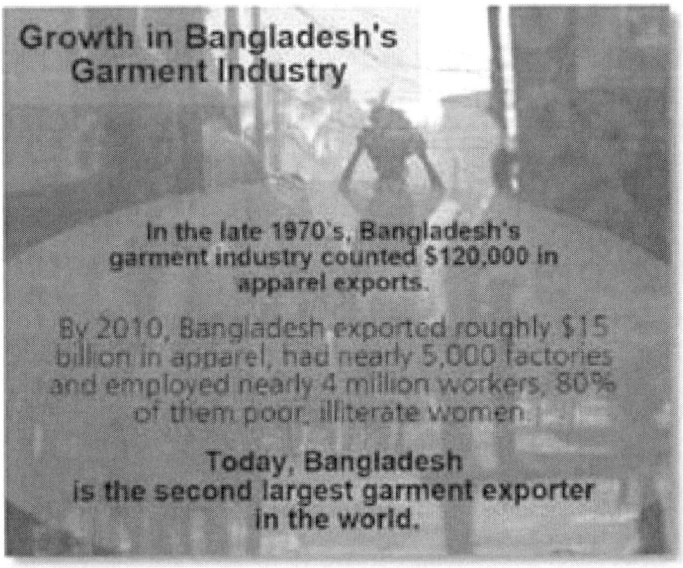

Although the suspension of Bangladesh's GSP trade benefits affected only a small portion of Bangladesh's exports to the United States (less than 1 percent), the action helped to focus the attention of the Bangladeshi Government on the measures it would need to take to improve worker rights and worker safety.

At the same time as the withdrawal, the Administration provided the Government of Bangladesh with an action plan that, if implemented, could provide a basis for the President to reinstate GSP benefits. The plan included specific commitments with respect to government inspections for labor, fire and building safety. The plan also included provisions regarding reforming labor law and practice to protect the rights to organize and collectively bargain in the apparel sector, export processing zones and the shrimp processing sector.

Since July 2013, the United States has also been working in partnership with the European Union, the ILO and the Government of Bangladesh under the "Sustainability Compact" on workers' rights and factory safety in the garment sector in Bangladesh to ensure a coordinated approach to improving labor conditions and respect for workers' rights in the sector. These efforts have also been matched with significant related technical assistance.

The Compact for Continuous Improvements in Labour Rights and Factory Safety in the Ready-Made Garment and Knitwear Industry in Bangladesh (Sustainability Compact) is a joint effort by the United States, European Union, International Labor Organization and Bangladesh, developed in the wake of the Rana Plaza tragedy, to address workers' rights and worker safety concerns in the Bangladeshi garment sector. The goals of the Sustainability Compact are broadly consistent with, and complement, those in the action plan that the United States developed in connection with its GSP program. The Sustainability Compact is an important public commitment by the Government of Bangladesh to undertake specific reforms and actions—with support from the United States, European Union, and ILO—to improve respect for workers' rights and workplace safety.

In October 2014, one and half years after the Rana Plaza collapse, the parties to the Sustainability Compact gathered in Brussels for a stocktaking meeting. The Compact partners acknowledged improvements since the launch of the Compact, such as increased union registrations and authorization for hiring of inspectors. However, the partners also "recognised that there are a number of areas where further measures need to be taken for full implementation of actions outlined in the Compact, with a view to sustaining progress made and securing further improvements in occupational safety and health, working conditions, and the respect for labour rights." This includes important outstanding work on labor law reforms and addressing unfair labor practices. The partners indicated their joint commitment to address the outstanding issues and have agreed to conduct a further review of the commitments in 2015.

Progress

U.S. and international efforts with Bangladesh have supported progress in some key areas:

- Amendments to Bangladesh Labour Act. With technical support of the ILO, funded in part by DOL, the Government of Bangladesh drafted and passed amendments to the Bangladesh Labour Act in July 2013. The amendments included a number of improvements sought by the ILO, including to permit the operation of a Better Work factory monitoring program in the garment sector, such as provisions to improve trade union registration procedures and expand access during collective bargaining to experienced negotiators.

- Some new inspectors hired. Since the collapse of Rana Plaza, the Inspectorate of Factories and Establishments has hired dozens of new inspectors and undertaken a concerted program for re-training on fire and building safety.
- Some fire, electrical, and structural safety inspections conducted. With assistance from the private sector—including the international brands and retailers participating in the so-called "Alliance" and "Accord" initiatives—over 2,000 factories, representing all of the major suppliers to North America and Europe, have been inspected by either government or third-party inspectors for fire, electrical and structural safety and the most urgent remediation measures have largely been completed.
- Website listing factories and posting inspection reports. The Ministry of Labour and Employment (MOLE) has created a website listing approximately 3,500 factories and begun posting summary inspection reports of the factories.

Remaining Challenges

Despite these improvements, much work remains to be done to implement the GSP Action Plan and Sustainability Compact and improve worker safety and respect for workers' rights.

- Regulations implementing the amendments to Bangladesh Labour Act. Bangladesh has not yet issued regulations implementing the July 2013 amendments to the Bangladesh Labour Act.
- Government delays in completing inspections and hiring additional inspectors. The most recent U.S. Government review of progress on the GSP Action Plan found that the Government of Bangladesh is behind schedule in carrying out hundreds of critical safety inspections and in hiring additional inspectors.
- Slow response to unfair labor practices. While the Government of Bangladesh has, for the first time, undertaken a number of investigations and prosecutions of unfair labor practices, it has been slow to offer protections for labor activists, particularly those organizing unions, and labor law enforcement remains inadequate.
- Labor reforms for export processing zones. The United States continues to press Bangladesh to pass other needed labor law reforms, including for export processing zones.

The U.S. Government has underscored that progress in these and other areas is critical to ensuring the safety of workers and their ability to exercise their fundamental rights to organize and collectively bargain. On June 14, 2014, U.S. Trade Representative Froman met with Commerce Minister Tofail Ahmed to urge the Government of Bangladesh to take further actions pursuant to the Action Plan and Sustainability Compact.

In October 2014, Ambassador Froman also met with Bangladesh's Ambassador to the United States, Mohammad Ziauddin, in advance of a periodic review of Bangladesh's efforts under the Action Plan, to urge further progress.

Looking Ahead

We remain committed to working with Bangladesh to address fully the outstanding concerns about workers' rights and worker safety. Our interest, and that of our international partners, remains as strong today as it was in the aftermath of the terrible Tazreen and Rana Plaza tragedies. The lessons from those tragedies continue to inform our work not only in Bangladesh, but in other parts of the world.

SWAZILAND

KEY EXPORTS TO THE UNITED STATES:
Knit and woven apparel, prepared fruits and vegetables

LABOR FORCE:
424,100 workers

RELEVANT TRADE POLICY TOOLS:
African Growth and Opportunity Act (AGOA)

Overview

Swaziland is a beneficiary of the African Growth and Opportunity Act (AGOA). AGOA offers regional preferences for qualified sub-Saharan African countries that build on the GSP program and provide additional market access to the United States, including for apparel. AGOA has its own set of eligibility criteria that sub-Saharan African countries must meet in order to enjoy its benefits. One of these criteria is that sub-Saharan countries must have "established" or be making "continual progress toward establishing" protection of internationally recognized worker rights, including the right to organize and bargain collectively.

For a number of years, the U.S. Government has conveyed to the Swazi Government serious concerns about labor conditions in Swaziland. Specifically, the U.S. Government has expressed concern about respect for workers' rights to assembly and association and to form trade unions, including Swaziland's use of security forces and arbitrary arrests to stifle peaceful demonstrations and the lack of legal recognition for worker and employer federations. The United States has repeatedly conveyed that these actions raise questions about the country's compliance with the AGOA labor criteria.

These concerns have grown in recent years. As the State Department's 2013 Human Rights Report notes, in April 2012, the Government deregistered the Trade Union Congress of Swaziland labor federation, claiming that the Swazi Industrial Relations Act only permitted registration of "organizations," not "federations." Additionally, the Government conducted police raids of trade union headquarters, detained and threatened union leaders and committed other acts of apparent intimidation that violated workers' right to freedom of association.

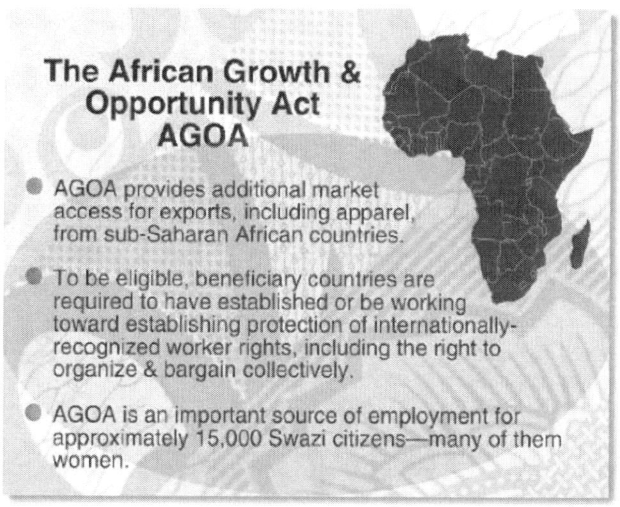

In response, the United States identified five discrete, short-term benchmarks that the Swazi Government could meet to address the labor concerns and offered to provide Swaziland assistance in satisfying them. Specifically, the United States urged Swaziland to make concrete and measurable progress in the following areas:

- Amendment of the Swazi Industrial Relations Act to allow for the registration of worker and employer federations.

- Amendment of the Swazi Suppression of Terrorism Act to ensure that the definition of terrorism does not undermine the rights to freedom of association, assembly, speech and to organize.
- Amendment of the Swazi Industrial Relations Act to remove any civil or criminal liability for participants in peaceful labor protests.
- Amendment of the Swazi Public Order Act to ensure that provisions to protect public order do not undermine the rights to freedom of association, assembly, speech and to organize.
- Approval, dissemination, and implementation of a Swazi Code of Good Practice on Protest and Industrial Action, in conformity with international standards.

In April 2014, an interagency U.S. Government delegation traveled to Swaziland to assess progress in meeting these benchmarks and to meet with senior Swazi Government officials, parliamentarians, civil society representatives, private sector stakeholders and trade union representatives to urge compliance by Swaziland.

In June 2014, faced with the lack of any progress toward meeting the five benchmarks, President Obama made the decision to withdraw benefits for Swaziland under AGOA, effective January 1, 2015. The withdrawal of trade benefits from Swaziland represented the first-ever such action under the AGOA program for violations of the workers' rights criteria.

The decision was not taken without careful consideration. Swaziland is one of the smallest countries in sub-Saharan Africa, with high rates of poverty and unemployment and one of the highest HIV/AIDS prevalence rates in the world. AGOA has been a major boon to the Swazi apparel sector, which is an important source of employment for approximately 15,000 Swazi citizens, many of them women.

However, after extensive U.S. Government efforts to encourage reform failed to achieve progress, it became clear that the Swazi Government lacked the political will to bring about basic changes necessary to protect internationally recognized workers' rights, which are both integral to the AGOA framework and critical to ensuring sustainable, broad-based economic growth.

Looking Ahead

The Administration considers the suspension of AGOA benefits as a means to help bring about much-needed change on the ground and will continue to engage with the Government of Swaziland on the issue of workers' rights. On August 7, 2014, U.S. Trade Representative Froman met with King Mswati III of Swaziland and, separately, with representatives of the Swazi labor movement to discuss AGOA and the importance of the Government and stakeholders working together to ensure that Swaziland takes the actions necessary to regain benefits under the program. The U.S. Embassy in Swaziland also continues to engage with stakeholders and the Swazi Government to monitor labor conditions closely and press for further progress.

By the end of 2014, these efforts were beginning to bear some fruit. To address two of the five AGOA-related benchmarks, the Swazi Government passed legislation in November 2014 amending the Industrial Relations Act to allow for the registration of union federations and to remove a provision establishing criminal liability for labor leaders during peaceful demonstrations. The U.S. Government, working in close cooperation with stakeholders, will continue to press the Swazi Government to implement these reforms in a manner consistent with international standards, as well as to make the additional changes necessary to regain AGOA benefits.

HAITI

KEY EXPORTS TO THE UNITED STATES:
Knit and woven apparel, mangos, perfumery

LABOR FORCE:
4,810,000 workers

RELEVANT TRADE POLICY TOOLS:
Haiti Hemispheric Opportunity through Partnership Encouragement (HOPE) Act

Overview

Haiti is the poorest and only least-developed country in the Western Hemisphere, with 80 percent of the population living under the poverty line and 54 percent in abject poverty. More than two-thirds of Haiti's labor force does not have formal employment. In 2010, the official unemployment rate was nearly 41 percent. In 2012, 76 percent of Haiti's exports were to the United States.

The Haitian Hemispheric Opportunity through Partnership Encouragement Act (HOPE) program, originally passed by Congress in 2006 and updated in 2008 and 2010, provides critical opportunities for Haitian exports and jobs. It also establishes one of the most robust mechanisms under any U.S. trade program for monitoring and reporting on labor rights compliance.

Like AGOA, the HOPE program provides duty-free access to the U.S. market—including for important product categories like apparel—if Haiti meets certain eligibility criteria. Under HOPE, however, key labor eligibility requirements must be implemented at not just the national level, but the factory level as well. Specifically, factories exporting under the program are required to comply with core international labor standards and related Haitian labor laws. If a problem is identified and a factory does not remediate it, the factory can lose its duty-free access to the U.S. market.

In assessing factories' compliance with the labor criteria, the U.S. Government considers the factory-specific monitoring and assessments conducted by the ILO in Haiti pursuant to its Better Work program. Under Better Work, which promotes respect for labor rights and improved working conditions in global supply chains, the ILO inspects 100 percent of HOPE-eligible factories for compliance with fundamental labor standards and Haitian labor laws and publishes compliance reports for individual factories on a bi-annual basis.

Progress

Active monitoring of apparel factories, including through regular engagement with stakeholders and factory-specific and sector-wide technical and capacity building assistance from DOL and the ILO has helped bring about important progress in a number of areas. For example:

- Currently, there are six union confederations in the apparel sector, with affiliated members in over half of Haiti's apparel factories. In 2010, there was only one apparel factory in Haiti with a trade union presence.

- DOL has investigated allegations of labor violations at the factory level, identified factories that are not compliant with HOPE labor eligibility criteria and successfully facilitated remediation, including reinstatement of wrongly-terminated workers.

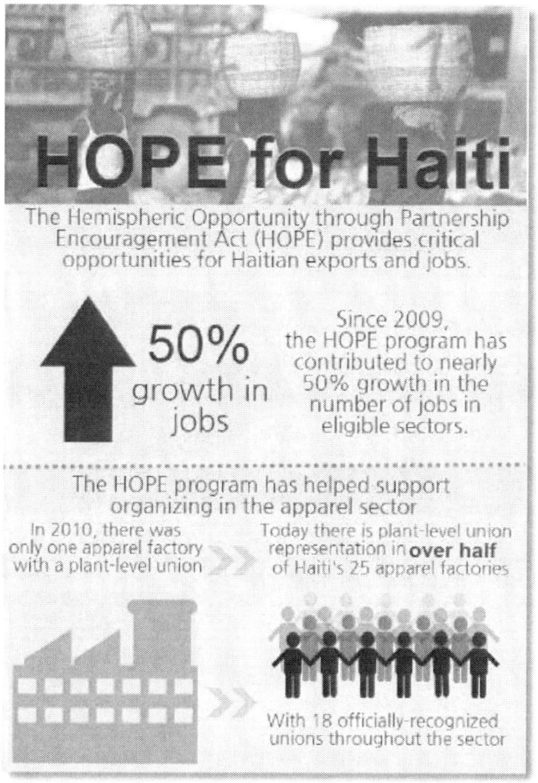

- Cases in which apparel factory managers require excessive and involuntary overtime by workers have dropped significantly.
- DOL has provided significant direct technical assistance in factories to improve compliance with international standards, including in particularly problematic areas, such as anti-union discrimination, forced overtime, and sexual harassment of female garment workers.

The ILO's Better Work Program monitors and reports on compliance by factories with fundamental labor standards, national labor laws consistent with those standards, and national laws on minimum wages, hours of work, and occupational safety and health. Better Work currently operates in a number of countries around the world: Cambodia (where the program got its start and is known as "Better Factories"), Haiti, Indonesia, Jordan, Lesotho, Nicaragua, and Vietnam. In Haiti, the program has a unique relationship to U.S. trade policy. The HOPE Act of 2008 required the Haitian Government to work with its own business and labor communities to develop a monitoring and compliance program operated by the ILO for those factories participating in the HOPE preference program. The Better Work Haiti program implements the mandate in the HOPE legislation.

Looking Ahead

Work continues across Haiti's apparel sector to help ensure compliance with fundamental labor standards and labor laws, particularly with respect to anti-union discrimination and sexual harassment, where significant challenges remain. This includes continued monitoring of factory-level compliance by DOL and Better Work Haiti, as well as significant direct technical assistance. DOL will continue to fund capacity building programming, including through projects aimed at improving the limited capacity of the Haitian ministry of labor, in particular the labor inspectorate and alternative dispute resolution systems, to help implement the provisions of the HOPE legislation and improve protection of worker rights and working conditions in Haiti's apparel sector.

BURMA

KEY EXPORTS TO THE UNITED STATES:
Fish and seafood, precious stones, artificial flowers, vegetables, knit apparel

LABOR FORCE:
34,130,000 workers

RELEVANT TRADE POLICY TOOLS:
Initiative to Promote Fundamental Labor Rights and Practices in Myanmar

Overview

Burma does not have a free trade agreement with the United States. Nor is Burma currently enjoying benefits under any preference program, having lost its GSP eligibility in July 1989 for non-compliance with the workers' rights criteria. The Obama Administration is however working with Burma to develop new tools to help Burma address labor rights issues and set a strong foundation for sustainable growth and development.

Burma is at a pivotal stage of its political and economic development. Its future depends on its ability to grow its economy, create good jobs and reintegrate into the global economy. Burma's ability to accomplish these goals—including by attracting substantial investment and fostering trade—is contingent on undertaking needed legal and economic reforms and on demonstrating that it is in good standing in the global community by respecting international human rights and fundamental labor standards. While Burma is certainly not the only country that faces these challenges, it has a unique opportunity to become a model for others by promoting strong labor laws, positive industrial relations in which workers' rights are respected and a competent, effective labor regulatory system at an early stage of its economic reform and development.

On August 28, 2014, during a visit by Ambassador Froman to Burma, the first ever by a U.S. Trade Representative, the United States and Burma announced that they would work together to establish a partnership to advance labor rights and protections for workers in Burma. On November 13, 2013, during a visit of President Obama to Burma, the initiative was formally launched by the United States, Burma, Japan, Denmark and the ILO. The United States is working to encourage the participation of other governments as well as the initiative develops.

Known as the *Initiative to Promote Fundamental Labor Rights and Practices in Myanmar*, the program takes a multilateral, multi-stakeholder approach to strengthen labor reform, enforcement, transparency and domestic stakeholder consultations. It is supported by two pillars.

- PILLAR 1: Development by the Burmese Government, in partnership with the ILO and other governments, of a multi-year labor reform plan. Burma has already undertaken some significant labor law reforms, but the labor reform plan will build on those legal reforms, helping Burma progress towards compliance with international standards, and will lay out a plan to improve the capacity of the Government to implement these reforms.

- PILLAR 2: Bringing stakeholders into the discussion on labor reforms and to help build the foundations for good industrial relations and civil society consultations in Burma. Specifically, the Initiative envisions the establishment of a stakeholder consultative mechanism that will foster tripartite engagement in Burma (among the Government, employers and workers), as well as engagement with civil society and build relations among international stakeholders from business, labor and civil society engaged in Burma.

Progress

Burma has already begun moving forward on the first pillar of the Initiative. Under an ILO-supported donor coordination mechanism known as the Nay Pyi Taw Accord, Burma has established a specific working group technical cluster on labor law reform and labor law enforcement capacity building that will be used to develop the labor reform plan. The first meeting of this working group was held on October 16, 2014. DOL is providing initial "seed" funding to the ILO in order to bring on board a labor law expert to assist the Government in developing the labor reform plan over the next six months through this working group.

The United States is also working to engage the international community to support this work. On October 10, 2014, U.S. Trade Representative Froman brought together representatives from the United States, Burma, Australia, the

European Union, Japan, the Netherlands, Norway, Sweden, as well as the ILO, the World Bank and the International Finance Corporation to discuss supporting the Labor Initiative.

Looking Ahead

While the initiative is still in early development stages, key benchmarks will include the development and passage of labor legislation that is consistent with international standards, regular consultations between business and labor interests, as well as civil society and concrete, significant improvements in the capacity of the Government to enforce labor laws and ensure that Burma's growth supports its goals of sustainable and inclusive economic development.

LABOR PROTECTIONS

1994 → *2014*

	NAFTA	Jordan	Singapore Chile Australia Morocco CAFTA-DR Bahrain Oman	Peru Colombia Korea Panama	Trans-Pacific Partnership
Labor provisions in the core of the agreement.	✗	✓	✓	✓	✓
Parties must adopt and maintain fundamental labor rights	✗	✗	✗	✓	✓
Parties must not waive or derogate from laws implementing fundamental labor rights	✗	✗	✗	✓	✓
Parties must adopt and maintain statutes and regulations governing acceptable conditions of work	✗	✗	✗	✗	✓
Parties shall take measures to discourage importation of goods made by forced labor	✗	✗	✗	✗	✓
Parties shall not waive or derogate from *any* labor laws if it would weaken labor protections in export processing zones	✗	✗	✗	✗	✓
Parties must effectively enforce their own labor laws	✓	✓	✓	✓	✓
Normal dispute settlement applies to all labor provisions	✗	✓	✗	✓	✓
Normal trade sanctions apply to all labor provisions	✗	✓	✗	✓	✓

TPP & T-TIP

The Obama Administration is not only using existing trade policy tools to improve respect for fundamental workers' rights and working conditions in our trading partners; we are developing stronger tools with even greater reach. With the Trans-Pacific Partnership (TPP) agreement with 11 countries in the Asia-Pacific region (Australia, Brunei Darussalam, Canada, Chile, Japan, Malaysia, Mexico, New Zealand, Peru, Singapore and Vietnam) and the Transatlantic Trade and Investment Partnership negotiations (T-TIP) with the 28 Members of the European Union, we are seeking to build on existing agreements and negotiate the strongest FTA labor protections in history. When completed, these agreements—and the protections provided under them—will apply to nearly two-thirds of the global economy.

TPP and T-TIP bear very little resemblance to early trade agreements like NAFTA. Indeed, NAFTA did not include any labor provisions—those were included in a side agreement known as the North American Agreement on Labor Cooperation or "NAALC." Only a single provision of the NAALC—the obligation to effectively enforce parties' own occupational safety and health, child labor and minimum wage technical labor standards—could be the subject of dispute settlement. Further, the dispute settlement processes and sanctions for violations of the NAALC were not the same as for the provisions of NAFTA. For example, a violation of the former could generally only be remedied through the imposition of an annual monetary assessment (a fine) subject to a cap, whereas violations of NAFTA could be subject to broad "suspension of concessions" (imposition of tariffs on the violating party's exports) until the violating party came into compliance.

The labor provisions in U.S. free trade agreements have evolved significantly since NAFTA. With the free trade agreement with Jordan, labor provisions were brought into the core of trade agreements. But the key operative discipline in the U.S.-Jordan FTA continued to be an "enforce your own law" standard and parties were only required to "strive" towards other goals, such as ensuring compliance with internationally recognized labor standards in law and practice.

It was not until the "May 10, 2007" bipartisan Congressional-Executive Agreement that a breakthrough was made in that regard, with critical new labor obligations relating to fundamental labor rights being made subject to full dispute settlement and normal trade sanctions. The "May 10" provisions were included, for the first time, in the free trade agreement with Peru and, thereafter, Colombia, Panama and South Korea.

These "May 10" provisions have been the starting point of the Obama Administration's labor negotiations in TPP. Including the groundbreaking "May 10" provisions in TPP means that countries will be expected to "adopt and maintain" in their laws and practices the fundamental labor rights as stated in the ILO Declaration on Fundamental Principles and Rights at Work. Workers must have the right to organize, to bargain collectively, to be free from forced labor and child labor and to be free from discrimination in employment. If a country fails to implement those fundamental rights, it can be held accountable through the dispute settlement processes set out in the agreements.

But the "May 10" provisions have not been a ceiling. In TPP, we are seeking new commitments to discourage trade in goods produced by forced labor, to adopt and maintain laws on acceptable working conditions (e.g., minimum wage, maximum hours and occupational health and safety), and not to weaken labor protections in export processing zones.

T-TIP also presents a unique opportunity to raise the bar on labor. The European Union and United States have some of the highest labor standards in the world. T-TIP provides an opportunity for these two major players to develop a framework that not only reflects their own high labor standards but strengthens their collective capacity to address labor concerns in the dozens of developing countries whose largest trade and investment relationships are with the United States and the EU.

Simply put—with T P P and T -TIP—we have a real opportunity t o lock i n the gains w e have made i n recent years t o protect workers' rights, improve working conditions, shape globalization and level the global playing field for American workers.

MAKING A DIFFERENCE

The common thread across all of the countries, programs and initiatives highlighted throughout this report is that trade policy tools can be used—and, under the Obama Administration, are being used—to support the aspirations of workers in this country and in trading partner countries around the world to earn a decent living in a safe and healthy workplace, enjoy fundamental labor rights and share in growing prosperity. Where we can, we need to strengthen our hand and extend our reach to achieve these ends. And the disciplines that the United States is negotiating in TPP, and will seek in T-TIP, will help us do that –calling for respect for fundamental labor rights for two-thirds of the world's economy and helping to establish a new norm for protecting workers' rights in the global trading system.

As President Obama has made clear, U.S. trade policy must be consistent with both our interests and our values. The clarity and consistency of that commitment is at the heart of efforts by USTR, DOL and other U.S. agencies to protect workers' rights. By defending the dignity of workers abroad, we are helping to ensure that trade-driven growth is inclusive and broad-based. We are also helping to level the global playing field for American workers. U.S. trade policy can, and must, work for workers at home and around the world.

USTR OVERVIEW

The Office of the United States Trade Representative (USTR) is responsible for developing, negotiating and coordinating U.S. international trade and investment policy.

Established in 1962, the Office of the United States Trade Representative provides trade policy leadership and negotiating expertise in areas including bilateral, regional and multilateral trade and investment issues, expansion of market access for American goods and services, negotiations affecting U.S. import policies, oversight of U.S. preference programs, trade-related intellectual property protection issues and World Trade Organization (WTO) issues.

USTR is part of the Executive Office of the President and the head of USTR, the U.S. Trade Representative, is a Cabinet member who serves as the principal trade advisor, negotiator and spokesperson on trade issues.

DOL OVERVIEW

The Bureau of International Labor Affairs (ILAB) leads the U.S. Department of Labor's efforts to ensure that workers around the world are treated fairly and are able to share in the benefits of the global economy. ILAB's mission is to improve global working conditions, raise living standards, protect workers' ability to exercise their rights and address the workplace exploitation of children and other vulnerable populations. ILAB's efforts help to ensure a fair global playing field for American workers and contribute to stronger export markets for goods made in the United States.

ILAB's Office of Trade and Labor Affairs (OTLA) engages in the drafting, negotiation, monitoring and enforcement of the labor provisions of U.S. free trade agreements; the administration of the labor eligibility criteria of U.S. trade preference programs; the development and implementation of trade- and investment-related international labor policy; and the coordination, funding and oversight of international technical assistance projects and cooperation to improve respect for workers' rights, livelihoods and labor law enforcement and compliance in U.S. trading partners.

In: Protecting Workers' Rights ...
Editor: Samuel T. Stokes

ISBN: 978-1-63483-176-5

Chapter 2

FREE TRADE AGREEMENTS: U.S. PARTNERS ARE ADDRESSING LABOR COMMITMENTS, BUT MORE MONITORING AND ENFORCEMENT ARE NEEDED*

United States Government Accountability Office

WHY GAO DID THIS STUDY

The United States has signed 14 FTAs, liberalizing U.S. trade with 20 countries. These FTAs include provisions regarding fundamental labor rights in the partner countries. USTR and DOL, supported by State, are responsible for monitoring and assisting FTA partners' implementation of these provisions.

GAO was asked to assess the status of implementation of FTA labor provisions in partner countries. GAO examined (1) steps that selected partner countries have taken, and U.S. assistance they have received, to implement these provisions and other labor initiatives and the reported results of such steps; (2) submissions regarding possible violations of FTA labor provisions that DOL has accepted and any problems related to the submission process; and (3) the extent to which U.S. agencies monitor and enforce implementation

* This is an edited, reformatted and augmented version of a United States Government Accountability Office publication, No. GAO-15-160, dated November 2014.

of FTA labor provisions and report results to Congress. GAO selected CAFTA-DR and the FTAs with Colombia, Oman, and Peru as representative of the range of FTAs with labor provisions, among other reasons. GAO reviewed documentation related to each FTA and interviewed U.S., partner government, and other officials in five of the partner countries.

WHAT GAO RECOMMENDS

DOL should reevaluate its submission review time frame and better inform stakeholders about the submission process. USTR and DOL should establish a coordinated strategic approach to monitoring and enforcement labor provisions. USTR's annual report to Congress should include more information of USTR's and DOL's monitoring and enforcement efforts. The agencies generally agreed with the recommendations but disagreed with some findings, including the finding that they lack a systematic approach to monitor and enforce labor provisions in all FTAs. GAO stands by its findings.

WHAT GAO FOUND

Partner countries of free trade agreements (FTA) that GAO selected—the Dominican Republic-Central America-United States Free Trade Agreement (CAFTA-DR) and the FTAs with Colombia, Oman, and Peru—have taken steps to implement labor provisions and other initiatives to strengthen labor rights. For example, U.S. and foreign officials said that El Salvador and Guatemala—both partners to CAFTA-DR—as well as Colombia, Oman, and Peru have acted to change labor laws, and Colombia and Guatemala have acted to address violence against union members. Since 2001, U.S. agencies have provided $275 million in labor-related technical assistance and capacity-building activities for FTA partners, including $222 million for the four FTAs GAO reviewed. However, U.S. agencies reported, and GAO found, persistent challenges to labor rights, such as limited enforcement capacity, the use of subcontracting to avoid direct employment, and, in Colombia and Guatemala, violence against union leaders.

Since 2008, the Department of Labor (DOL) has accepted five formal complaints—known as submissions—about possible violations of FTA labor provisions and has resolved one, regarding Peru (see fig.). However, for each submission, DOL has exceeded by an average of almost 9 months its 6-month time frame for investigating FTA-related labor submissions and issuing public reports, showing the time frame to be unrealistic. Also, union representatives and other stakeholders GAO interviewed in partner countries often did not understand the submission process, possibly limiting the number of submissions filed. Further, stakeholders expressed concerns that delays in resolving the submissions, resulting in part from DOL's exceeding its review time frames, may have contributed to the persistence of conditions that affect workers and are allegedly inconsistent with the FTAs.

FTA	Year accepted	Alleged violations	Status
Bahrain	2011	Violation of right to freedom of association, discrimination	Open
Dominican Republic	2012	Human trafficking, forced labor, retaliatory firing of workers for union activities	Open
Guatemala	2008	Violation of right to freedom of association, violation of rights to organize and bargain collectively, unacceptable work conditions	Open
Honduras	2012	Violation of right to freedom of association, violations of rights to organize and bargain collectively, child labor	Open
Peru	2011	Failure to comply with labor laws related to collective bargaining	Closed as resolved (2012)

Source: GAO analysis of Department of Labor (DOL) information. | GAO-15-160.

Five Labor Submissions Accepted by DOL Regarding Free Trade Agreements.

In 2009, GAO found weaknesses in the Office of the U.S. Trade Representative's (USTR) and DOL's monitoring and enforcement of FTA labor provisions. In the same year, the agencies pledged to adopt a more proactive, interagency approach. GAO's current review found that although the agencies have taken several steps since 2009 to strengthen their monitoring and enforcement of FTA labor provisions, they lack a strategic approach to systematically assess whether partner countries' conditions and practices are inconsistent with labor provisions in the FTAs. Despite some proactive steps, they generally rely on labor submissions to begin identifying, investigating, and initiating steps to address possible inconsistencies with FTA labor provisions. According to agency officials, resource limitations have prevented more proactive monitoring of all FTA labor provisions. As a result, USTR and DOL systematically monitor and enforce compliance with FTA labor provisions for only a few priority countries. USTR's annual report to Congress about trade agreement programs provides limited details of the results of the agencies' monitoring and enforcement of compliance with FTA labor provisions.

ABBREVIATIONS

AFL-CIO	American Federation of Labor and Congress of Industrial Organizations
CAFTA-DR	Dominican Republic-Central America-United States Free Trade Agreement
CICIG	International Commission against Impunity in Guatemala
DOL	Department of Labor
DPPS	División de Protección de Personas y Seguridad
DRL	Bureau of Democracy, Human Rights, and Labor
ENS	Escuela Nacional Sindical
FTA	free trade agreement
ILO	International Labour Organization
INL	Bureau of International Narcotics and Law Enforcement
NAFTA	North American Free Trade Agreement
NGO	nongovernmental organization
SENA	Servicio Nacional de Aprendizaje
SINAUT	National Union of Tax Administration Workers
SUNAUT	National Superintendency of Tax Administration
TPSC	Trade Policy Staff Committee
UNP	Unidad Nacional de Protección
USAID	U.S. Agency for International Development
USTR	Office of the U.S. Trade Representative

* * *

November 6, 2014

The Honorable George Miller
Ranking Member
Committee on Education and the Workforce
House of Representatives

The Honorable Sander M. Levin
Ranking Member
Committee on Ways and Means
House of Representatives

As global economic competition has intensified, concerns in the United States that competitors' labor practices may disadvantage U.S. workers and producers have become acute. Recent U.S. free trade agreements (FTA) contain a provision requiring partner countries to commit to respect internationally accepted core labor rights, such as freedom of association and the right to bargain collectively.[1] FTAs phase out barriers to trade with particular countries or groups of countries and contain rules and other commitments to improve access for services and investment. FTAs represent a major component of U.S. trade policy, as the United States has signed 14 FTAs with 20 countries covering, according to the Department of Commerce, more than 35 percent of all U.S. imports—$2.3 trillion in 2013.[2] The status of the implementation of FTA labor provisions is of particular relevance, as the United States is negotiating the Trans-Pacific Partnership—a trade agreement with 11 Pacific Rim countries, in which the administration is seeking to negotiate high-standard labor provisions. The effective implementation of labor provisions is also relevant as Congress considers renewal of the President's lapsed Trade Promotion Authority, most recently in effect from 2002 through 2007.[3]

In 2009, we reported significant challenges connected with the enforcement of labor provisions in four FTAs.[4] We also reported that the U.S. agencies responsible for the monitoring and implementation of labor provisions in the FTAs in many cases engaged in only minimal oversight and assistance with FTA partner countries to address these challenges. We recommended that the Department of Labor (DOL), in consultation with other agencies, initiate regular contact with all FTA partners' ministries of labor to review implementation of FTA labor provisions and to develop ongoing priorities and plans for technical cooperation on labor matters. We also recommended that the Office of the U.S. Trade Representative (USTR), in cooperation with other agencies, prepare updated plans to implement, enforce, monitor, and report on compliance with and progress under the FTAs' labor provisions and that these plans should reflect ongoing trade developments, be provided to Congress, and be summarized in USTR's annual trade agreements report. In 2012, both agencies were taking actions to address the recommendations.[5]

As the main U.S. point of contact for all FTAs, USTR has general oversight responsibility for commitments in FTAs. DOL is responsible for monitoring partner countries' labor conditions and compliance with FTA labor provisions, addressing complaints regarding violations of these provisions, and providing technical assistance. The Department of State (State) supports USTR and DOL in discharging their responsibilities and also monitors labor conditions in each partner country. In some instances, the U.S. Agency for International Development (USAID) supports partner countries in implementing FTA labor obligations and initiatives by administering technical assistance projects, carried out by USAID's implementing partners. In 2009, USTR announced that it would take steps jointly with DOL and State to improve interagency cooperation; proactively monitor the implementation of labor provisions; and address identified problem areas, including foreign practices that would constitute violations of FTA requirements. Furthermore, the President's 2014 Trade Policy Agenda indicates that the administration will focus on implementation of the numerous agreements into which the United States has entered and that the United States will work with key trading partners around the world to address specific labor issues.

You asked us to assess the current status of the implementation of FTA labor provisions as well as the United States' and trade partner countries' responses to related challenges, such as reported violence against unionists in some partner countries. This report examines the following (see app. I for a detailed description of our scope and methodology):

1) steps that selected partner countries have taken, and U.S. assistance they have received, to implement FTA labor provisions and other labor initiatives and the reported results of such steps;
2) complaints—known as submissions—about possible violations of FTA labor provisions that DOL has accepted and any problems related to the submission process; and
3) the extent to which USTR, DOL, and State monitor and enforce partner countries' implementation of FTA labor provisions and report results to Congress.

In addition, appendix II describes reported violence against labor unionists in selected FTA partner countries as well as steps that the countries have taken to address such occurrences. Appendix III describes U.S. agencies' efforts to monitor implementation of other labor initiatives.

For our review, we selected four FTAs—the Dominican Republic-Central America-United States Free Trade Agreement (CAFTA-DR), the United States-Colombia Trade Promotion Agreement (Colombia FTA), the United States-Oman Free Trade Agreement (Oman FTA), and the United States-Peru Trade Promotion Agreement (Peru FTA). We also visited five partner countries—El Salvador and Guatemala, both of which are CAFTA-DR partners; Colombia; Oman; and Peru. We selected these FTAs and countries in part because of the extent of known labor issues in each country; because of the timing of the FTAs' entry into force; and to reflect regional dispersion across Central America, South America, and the Middle East.[6] In addition, we selected the Colombia and Peru FTAs in part because the labor chapters in those agreements contain provisions reflecting labor language as delineated in the May 10, 2007, Bipartisan Trade Agreement on Trade Policy, popularly known as the May 10th Agreement.[7] However, the results of our review of these selected FTAs and partner countries cannot be generalized to all FTAs and partner countries.

To address our objectives, we reviewed relevant documents, including the labor chapters of the four selected FTAs; labor submissions received by DOL; labor rights reports and trade agreement reports compiled by U.S. agencies, international organizations, and FTA stakeholders; and documents pertaining to U.S. monitoring and enforcement plans. In addition, we reviewed documentation related to labor conditions in partner countries that we obtained from partner country governments as well as from business associations, labor unions, the International Labour Organization (ILO), and nonprofit organizations. We interviewed representatives of these organizations; relevant foreign government officials; and U.S. agency officials in Colombia, El Salvador, Guatemala, Oman, and Peru during fieldwork in those countries. We also interviewed U.S. agency representatives in Washington, D.C., and Geneva, Switzerland.[8] We collected data on U.S. funding for labor assistance programs in FTA partner countries from 2001 to 2013 and on reported violence against unionists in Colombia—the only selected FTA partner country with such data—and we assessed these data's reliability by interviewing agency officials knowledgeable about the data sources and by tracing the data to source documents. We determined that the data were sufficiently reliable for the purposes of describing U.S. assistance for implementation of labor provisions in FTA partner countries and describing general trends in reported violence against unionists in Colombia. (See app. I for further details of our scope and methodology.)

We conducted this performance audit from May 2013 to November 2014 in accordance with generally accepted government auditing standards. Those standards require that we plan and perform the audit to obtain sufficient, appropriate evidence to provide a reasonable basis for our findings and conclusions based on our audit objectives. We believe that the evidence obtained provides a reasonable basis for our findings and conclusions based on our audit objectives.

BACKGROUND

FTA Labor Provisions and Other Initiatives to Address Labor Concerns

The current and prior administrations have expressed concerns that poor labor standards in FTA partner countries may affect workers in the United States and other parts of the world, incentivizing a global "race to the bottom" that unfairly distorts global markets and prevents U.S. businesses and workers from competing on a level playing field. According to DOL, to address such concerns, each FTA signed in the past decade, including those we selected, contains a "labor chapter" that differs in detail across the FTAs but generally includes labor provisions, establishes points of contact for labor matters, and provides a recourse mechanism for matters arising from the labor provisions.[9] The provisions in the labor chapters of the four FTAs that took effect most recently generally reflect the trade policy template created by the May 10th Agreement.[10]

- In FTAs that entered into force from January 2004 through January 2009, including CAFTA-DR and the Oman FTA, the labor chapter contains a provision that a party shall not fail to effectively enforce its labor laws, through a sustained or recurring course of action or inaction, in a manner affecting trade between the parties.[11] Under CAFTA-DR and the Oman FTA, matters related to this obligation are the only matters under the respective labor chapters for which parties can seek recourse through dispute settlement that may result in possible fines and sanctions.[12] These FTAs also contain a provision whereby parties commit to "strive to ensure" that the labor rights enumerated in the respective labor chapter are protected by their laws;

however, matters arising under this provision do not have recourse through the dispute settlement chapter of the respective FTA.[13]

- In FTAs that entered into force after January 2009, including the Colombia and Peru FTAs,[14] the labor chapter includes language echoing the May 10th Agreement that obligates each partner to adopt and maintain in its statutes, regulations, and practices certain fundamental labor rights as stated by the ILO.[15] Although the text of the respective FTAs' labor chapters varies, this language generally relates to, for example, the rights to freedom of association and collective bargaining and the elimination of compulsory or forced labor. The labor chapters of these FTAs also obligate the parties not to fail to effectively enforce these labor laws in a manner affecting trade between the parties. Pursuant to the labor chapters of these FTAs, if consultations fail, the parties can seek to resolve matters arising under the labor chapters by pursuing recourse through the respective FTAs' dispute settlement chapters, which may result in possible fines and sanctions.[16]

In addition, other labor initiatives—one known as the White Paper[17] and the other titled *Colombian Action Plan Related to Labor Rights* (Labor Action Plan)[18]—were developed in the context of CAFTA-DR and the Colombia FTA, respectively.[19]

- **White Paper.** Before Congress enacted implementing legislation for CAFTA-DR,[20] a group of vice ministers responsible for trade and labor in the partner countries developed the White Paper to address labor concerns in Central America and the Dominican Republic. The White Paper detailed six areas of focus and included recommendations to enhance the implementation and enforcement of labor standards and to strengthen the region's labor institutions.[21] According to DOL, the U.S. government did not participate in preparing or negotiating the White Paper's recommendations. The ILO Verification Project, funded by DOL, was created to monitor implementation of the White Paper commitments and released verification reports every 6 months between 2007 and 2010.
- **Labor Action Plan.** Colombia and the United States agreed in 2011 to the Labor Action Plan, in furtherance of Colombia's commitment to protect internationally recognized labor rights, prevent violence against labor leaders, and prosecute the perpetrators of such violence.

The plan listed nine issue areas to strengthen labor rights that Colombia was required to address before the FTA could receive congressional approval. [22] USTR and DOL are jointly responsible for monitoring Colombia's ongoing progress in fulfilling these requirements.

U.S. Agencies' Responsibilities Related to Monitoring Implementation of FTA Labor Provisions

USTR, DOL, and State have key responsibilities related to monitoring partner countries' implementation of FTA labor provisions. These roles involve both discrete and shared responsibilities that require both formal and informal coordination. USAID has provided funding for cooperative projects to improve labor capacity.

- **USTR.** The U.S. Trade Representative is the President's principal adviser and spokesperson on trade and has lead responsibility for negotiating trade agreements, including FTAs, as well as for developing and coordinating U.S. trade policy and issuing policy guidance related to international trade functions. USTR is responsible to the President and Congress for administering the trade agreements program, including periodic reporting to Congress as required.[23] USTR is also responsible for coordinating the administration's activities to create a fair, open, and predictable trading environment by identifying, monitoring, enforcing, and resolving the full range of international trade issues. According to USTR, this includes asserting U.S. rights; vigorously monitoring and enforcing bilateral and other agreements; and promoting U.S. interests, including labor interests, under FTAs.
- **DOL.** DOL's Bureau of International Labor Affairs is responsible for monitoring implementation of FTA labor provisions for all FTAs. The bureau's Office of Trade and Labor Affairs is designated as the point of contact for implementation of the labor provisions of the FTAs as well as for the labor cooperation mechanisms. Before congressional approval and implementation of an FTA, DOL's responsibilities include preparing reports for Congress, in consultation with USTR and State, about the partner country's labor rights protections and child labor laws and the FTA's potential effect on employment in the

United States. After an FTA enters into force, DOL's responsibilities include receiving, reviewing, and acting on any public complaint submitted about the partner's compliance with FTA labor obligations (submissions). 24 Both before and after an FTA is implemented, DOL is responsible for assisting the partner country as needed—for example, planning, developing, and pursuing cooperative projects related to labor matters—to strengthen the partner country's capacity to promote respect for core labor standards.

- **State.** State is responsible for supporting USTR and DOL in implementing and monitoring FTAs. State's Bureau of Democracy, Human Rights, and Labor (DRL) coordinates State's in-country labor officers, who are tasked with carrying out regular monitoring and reporting and day-to-day interaction with foreign governments regarding labor matters. State annually produces *Country Reports on Human Rights Practices*, which includes information about countries' labor practices. In addition, State participates with USTR and DOL in the USTR-led interagency team that negotiates FTA labor provisions, contributes critical input to the research and analysis of reports produced by DOL, and provides technical assistance funding to strengthen some countries' labor capacity. Because USTR and DOL do not maintain a presence in other countries, they often rely on State for outreach, monitoring, and reporting activities related to FTA labor provisions.
- **USAID.** USAID administers technical assistance programs to address labor-related matters. USAID administers trade-capacity-building programs globally in both FTA and non-FTA partner countries. In addition, during the FTA negotiations, USAID provides USTR input on draft FTA text as well as input on possible trade-capacity-building programs to address labor-related issues.

Selected Countries Have Taken Steps, with U.S. Assistance, to Address FTA Labor Commitments and Other Labor Initiatives but Have Limited Enforcement Capacity

Each of the FTA partner countries that we selected for our review has taken steps to strengthen labor rights pursuant to its FTA with the United

States, and some of these countries have also implemented other labor initiatives outside the FTA framework. The U.S. government has provided some technical assistance to help FTA partner countries meet their labor commitments. However, stakeholders reported that limitations in partner countries' capacity to enforce labor laws cause gaps in labor protections to persist.

Selected Countries Have Taken Steps to Implement FTA Labor Commitments and Other Labor Initiatives, Including Strengthening Labor Institutions

CAFTA-DR: El Salvador and Guatemala

El Salvador and Guatemala, the CAFTA-DR countries we selected for our review, have both taken steps to implement labor initiatives responding to their FTA commitments and areas of focus identified in the White Paper. According to the ILO, and as reported by DOL, these countries have addressed these areas of focus by implementing changes to improve labor protections, such as increasing the number of labor inspectors and increasing the number of judges and courts that hear labor cases.

El Salvador

According to DOL and ILO verification reports, El Salvador increased its Ministry of Labor's enforcement budget by about 120 percent from 2005 to 2010, leading to an increase in the number of labor inspectors during the same period as well as increases in both the number of inspections conducted and the number of fines imposed on employers.[25] Ministry of Labor officials reported that with the increase in size and budget, which resulted from the White Paper recommendations, the ministry is now able to accommodate workers' requests for workplace inspections and labor inspectors can issue fines for violations not addressed by employers.[26] In addition, according to officials from the Supreme Court in El Salvador, the labor courts have created a comprehensive statistical system to track labor issues identified in the White Paper, and unions have successfully advocated for legislation that, if passed, would speed labor case reviews and allow plaintiffs to participate more actively.

Guatemala

Guatemala has taken some steps to address labor conditions in accordance with commitments outlined in an Enforcement Plan that the United States and Guatemala agreed to in 2013 as a result of negotiations to resolve a labor case initiated through a labor submission to DOL.[27] The actions that the plan calls for include, among others, increasing the budget for labor law enforcement at the Ministry of Labor and verifying employer compliance with court orders.[28] Officials from the Ministry of Labor reported improvements in labor rights implementation in response to the Enforcement Plan. For example, the number of labor inspections rose from about 5,000 nationwide in 2011 to about 36,800 nationwide in 2013. Also, according to ministry officials, the ministry now conducts labor inspections regularly, rather than in response to complaints, and has increased its legal education requirements for labor inspectors, to further fulfill its Enforcement Plan commitments.

Colombia

According to USTR, Colombia has taken steps to implement labor protection commitments outlined in the Labor Action Plan, such as reforming the criminal code to establish criminal penalties for employers that undermine the right to organize and bargain collectively, enacting legal provisions and regulations prohibiting the use of temporary service agencies to circumvent labor rights, and reforming the criminal justice system. USTR and DOL have reported that the Colombian government took concrete steps and made meaningful progress under the Labor Action Plan, which fulfilled the condition for advancing the FTA to Congress and resulted in the FTA's entering into force in May 2012. The government's steps included securing legislation to establish a separate labor ministry and expanding its labor inspectorate by hiring additional inspectors. Additionally, USTR and the Colombian Ministry of Labor reported that the government enacted a series of laws and ministerial decrees that expanded labor protections as a result of the Labor Action Plan. According to USTR and the Colombian Ministry of Labor, these laws and decrees include, for example, legislation to establish criminal penalties, including imprisonment, for employers that undermined the right to organize and bargain collectively as well as new provisions and regulations to prohibit and sanction with significant fines the misuse of cooperatives[29] and other employment relationships that undermine workers' rights.[30]

Oman

Oman has taken steps to implement labor protections that have allowed for unionization and collective bargaining. Officials from Oman's Ministry of Manpower—the ministry responsible for labor affairs—reported that Oman's interest in entering into a free trade agreement with the United States helped lead to the introduction of labor reforms, including the establishment of unions. According to USTR, in order to meet its commitments made in connection with the FTA, Oman has enacted a number of labor law reforms including, among others, a royal decree in 2006 that established the right to organize labor unions, allowed for collective bargaining, prohibited the dismissal of workers for union activity, guaranteed the right to strike, and guaranteed unions the right to practice their activities freely and without interference from outside parties. According to union and Ministry of Manpower officials we met with in Oman, the General Federation of Trade Unions held its first election in 2010 and served as the starting point for the union movement in Oman. The federation serves as an umbrella organization representing workers from various sectors and, according to union officials, represents about 200 company-level unions and one sector-level union, established in 2013 in the oil and gas sector.

Peru

According to USTR, Peru committed to steps to implement labor protection commitments in the context of FTA negotiations with the United States. During our fieldwork, officials at Peru's Ministry of Labor told us that Peru recently established a new labor inspection regime and that the ministry has focused on improving inspections in the workplace. For example, in 2013, according to Ministry of Labor officials, the ministry took action to centralize authority for labor inspections and help ensure that inspectors are applying the same criteria across the country. Ministry of Labor officials also reported that the ministry took steps to improve labor inspections by modernizing its information systems to allow for digital record keeping, with technical assistance provided by USAID. According to USAID, as a result of these programs, the time required to adjudicate labor cases has decreased from 2 years to 6 months. Additionally, according to a 2007 U.S. House of Representatives, Committee on Ways and Means report, in order to bring Peruvian labor laws into alignment with the obligations under the FTA, the government of Peru took steps to change Peru's legal framework governing temporary employment contracts, subcontracting and outsourcing contracts, the right of workers to strike, recourses against unit-union discrimination, and workers' right to organize. Ministry of Labor officials reported that the ministry has progressively increased the number of labor inspectors, in connection with the commitments Peru made during the FTA negotiation, to double its labor inspectorate. As of September 2013, the ministry reported having about 400 labor inspectors on staff nationally.

U.S. Agencies Have Provided Technical Assistance to Help FTA Partner Countries Meet Labor Commitments, with Largest Amounts for CAFTA-DR

From fiscal year 2001 through fiscal year 2013, the U.S. government provided a combined total of about $275 million in labor-related assistance for all FTA partner countries.[31] All CAFTA-DR countries, Colombia, and Peru received a combined total of about $222 million in labor-related technical assistance and capacity-building activities since the passage of implementing legislation for these FTAs. In contrast, the U.S. government provided about $53 million in labor-related assistance for all other FTA partner countries during the periods since those FTAs were implemented.[32]

Figure 1 shows the labor-related technical assistance that U.S. agencies provided under CAFTA-DR and the Colombia, Oman, and Peru FTAs during the periods beginning, respectively, with the year that Congress passed the FTA's implementing legislation and ending in 2013. Figure 1 also shows labor-related technical assistance that U.S. agencies provided from 2001 through 2013 under all other FTAs that entered into force in or after 2001.

CAFTA-DR

CAFTA-DR's six partner countries have received the largest amounts of U.S. assistance for labor-related projects undertaken pursuant to the FTA or independent of the FTA. From 2005, when the CAFTA-DR implementing legislation was passed by Congress, through 2013, the U.S. government provided about $170 million for such projects. According to DOL, this amount included funding appropriated by Congress to fund labor-capacity-building activities as well as funds appropriated to DOL for child labor technical assistance projects to assist these partner countries in addressing labor-related priorities outlined in the White Paper.[33] According to DOL officials, DOL, State, and USAID established an interagency group to develop FTA labor-related projects in consultation with USTR and CAFTA-DR partner governments and to allocate funding among these projects, with funds transferred from State. DOL reported that from 2005 to 2013, these three U.S. agencies administered more than 20 technical assistance projects in support of the White Paper's priority issue areas.

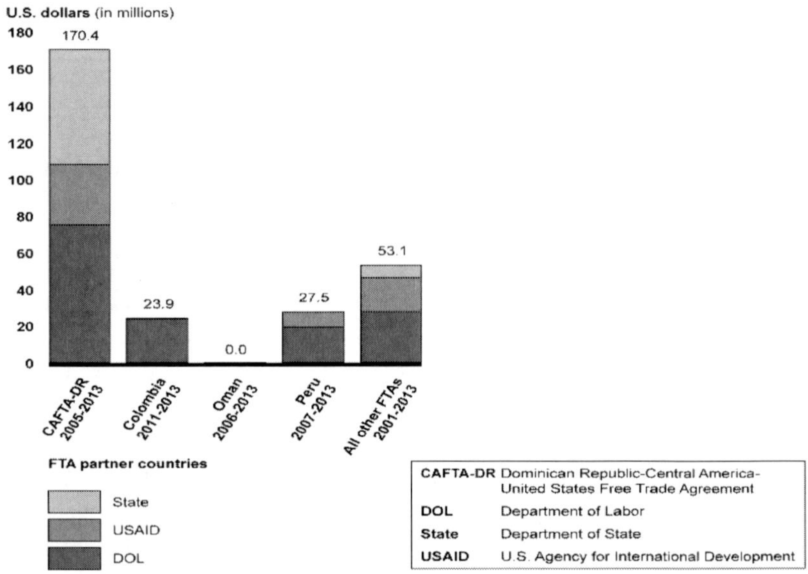

Source: GAO analysis of DOL, State, and USAID data. | GAO-15-160.

Notes: Time periods for the data shown for CAFTA-DR and the Colombia, Oman, and Peru FTAs each begin with the year that the respective FTA's implementing legislation was passed by Congress, before the FTA entered into force. Data for "All other FTAs" exclude the only FTAs that entered into force before 2001—the U.S.-Israel Free Trade Agreement (1985) and the North American Free Trade Agreement (1994).

Totals for projects that DOL administered under CAFTA-DR include projects that Congress funded through appropriations to DOL for technical assistance to reduce child labor as well as projects that State's Bureau of Western Hemisphere Affairs funded through transfers to DOL from State's Economic Support Fund and Development Assistance account.

Data shown exclude funding that DOL provided for a regional labor-related technical assistance project in Oman and Bahrain in 2006. According to DOL officials, data showing country-specific funding for regional projects are not available.

Data shown for Colombia include $500,000 that State provided for promotion of labor rights.

Figure 1. Labor-Related Technical Assistance Administered by U.S. Agencies under Selected Free Trade Agreements (FTA) and All Other FTAs.

Colombia

U.S. technical assistance for labor-related projects in Colombia totaled about $24 million from 2011, when the Colombia FTA implementing legislation was enacted, through 2013. U.S. agencies provided $9 million of that amount for projects to combat child labor and about $13 million to address workers' rights. DOL has also provided in-kind resources, sending a staff person with labor expertise to support the Colombian government in taking initial steps to implement the Labor Action Plan. The United States is currently funding multiple labor-related projects in Colombia, including State's award of about $500,000 to the ILO for the promotion of core labor rights and DOL's award of about $7.8 million for the ILO office in Colombia.

Oman

Oman has not received U.S. technical assistance specifically for labor-related projects since the FTA was enacted. According to State, the United States is not involved in any labor-capacity-building or labor-related assistance programs in Oman because of the Omani government's reluctance to accept foreign assistance. However, officials at Oman's Ministry of Manpower told us that the United States has provided information and advice on supporting unions and the role of unions in the economy and has expressed support of ongoing labor reforms, including the establishment of unions.

Peru

U.S technical assistance for labor-related projects in Peru totaled about $27.5 million from 2007, when the Peru FTA implementing legislation was enacted, through 2013. Of that amount, $13 million was dedicated to combat child labor, with the remainder dedicated to labor-capacitybuilding and education projects. USAID officials stated that, for example, the agency expended $3.3 million over a 3-year period to target labor issues. Of this amount, $2.7 million was granted to the Solidarity Center, a labor nongovernmental organization (NGO) affiliated with the American Federation of Labor and Congress of Industrial Organizations (AFL-CIO), to strengthen union negotiation capacity, and $600,000 was granted to an implementing partner—Nathan Associates—for improving information systems, providing training for labor inspectors, and training judges on the implementation of labor laws.

Stakeholders Reported Limited Enforcement Capacity and Gaps in Labor Rights in Selected Partner Countries

CAFTA-DR: El Salvador and Guatemala

El Salvador

Stakeholders we met with during our fieldwork in El Salvador identified concerns related to the enforcement of labor rights. Further, State and DOL reports show that workers are often unable to benefit from the legal rights afforded in the labor laws. For example, according to NGO officials, although labor courts have improved their ability to process cases, court decisions are often not enforced. U.S. officials stated that the Ministry of Labor's increases in its budget and number of labor inspectors have not improved the labor inspectorate's effectiveness. According to Ministry of Labor officials, although the ministry's labor inspectors can fine employers for labor law violations, the ministry does not collect the fines and workers must petition the labor courts to enforce the penalties. Moreover, according to an ILO official, although the government of El Salvador has greatly reduced the amount of time that the courts take to accept a case, resolution of most labor disputes still takes 2 to 4 years. Officials from the Supreme Court in El Salvador told us that about 51 percent of labor court sentences are not enforced, primarily because the plaintiffs do not have the funds required to continue the claims. Union and NGO officials we met with in El Salvador emphasized their concerns over enforcement, stating that because of the length of time the courts take to adjudicate labor cases, workers often take buyouts from the company and drop the cases. State's 2013 Human Rights Report echoes these concerns. For example, the report states that in 2013, the government of El Salvador did not always effectively enforce the laws on freedom of association and the right to collective bargaining, and that legal remedies and penalties are ineffective.

Guatemala

According to stakeholders we met with during our fieldwork in Guatemala, as well as State reports, concerns related to the enforcement and application of labor rights persist. According to USTR, Guatemala has taken steps to address labor reforms outlined in the Enforcement Plan, but additional steps are needed, including passing legislation providing for an expedited process to sanction employers that violate labor laws and implementing a mechanism to ensure payments to workers in cases where enterprises have closed.[34] Additionally, according to USTR, Guatemala will need to demonstrate that the legal reforms it has undertaken and still needs to undertake are being implemented effectively and are leading to positive changes.[35] Union representatives reported concerns related to freedom of association—specifically, that union leaders have been offered monetary compensation to resign from their jobs and to influence other workers against joining the union. Union officials we met with also noted that workers have been terminated for their union affiliation or for not disbanding unions. State's 2013 Human Rights Report echoed these concerns, stating that the government of Guatemala did not effectively enforce legislation on freedom of association, collective bargaining, or antiunion discrimination. Further, according to this report, as a result of inadequate allocation of budget resources and inefficient legal and administrative processes, the relevant government institutions did not effectively investigate, prosecute, and punish employers who violated freedom of association and collective bargaining laws, and the institutions did not reinstate workers illegally dismissed for engaging in union activities.[36]

Colombia

Stakeholders we met with in Colombia identified concerns related to the enforcement of labor rights and not benefiting from rights afforded in the labor laws. According to USTR, the government of Colombia has made meaningful progress under the Labor Action Plan, but work remains to build on this progress and address remaining and new challenges.

- According to USTR, the collection of fines for labor violations remains problematic. USTR and DOL have reported that although Colombia's national training and apprenticeship system, Servicio Nacional de Aprendizaje (SENA), is responsible for collecting fines for labor violations, until recently SENA has been barred from collecting fines from companies that filed a judicial appeal.[37] According to a joint USTR-DOL statement, as of April 2014, SENA was authorized to hold monetary payment as collateral payment from businesses, pending the outcome of the judicial appeal of their fines, but had not yet begun to exercise this authority. Additionally, although the Ministry of Labor increased the number of inspectors, labor unions and NGOs reported that this action has not resulted in more effective inspections or improved working conditions.
- USTR has reported that new forms of abusive contracting remain problematic to the protection of labor rights in Colombia. For example, according to USTR, although the number of illegal

> cooperatives has dropped, many employers have shifted to various forms of subcontracting, including entities known as simplified stock companies, to avoid direct employment relationships.[38] ILO, NGO, and labor union officials we met with described this form of subcontracting as a legal loophole that is used to undermine workers' rights. According to union officials, a law passed by the Colombian government in 2013 prohibiting the misuse of cooperatives was also intended to increase formalized employment and encourage companies to hire workers directly instead of as temporary labor.

State's 2013 Human Rights Report noted that the Colombian government generally enforced applicable labor laws and took steps to increase the enforcement of freedom-of-association laws. However, the report identified weaknesses in labor protections in Colombia, echoing concerns expressed to us by labor union and NGO representatives, related to labor inspections, collecting fines for labor violations, and employers' use of outsourcing contracts.[39]

Oman

Ministry of Manpower and union officials we met with in Oman reported that collective bargaining and freedom of association are allowed by law and largely respected. However, State has raised concerns about the enforcement of labor law among Oman's foreign worker population. State's 2013 Human Rights Report notes that Oman's Ministry of Manpower effectively enforces the labor law as it applies to Omani citizens but has not effectively enforced regulations related to working conditions and hours for foreign workers.

Peru

Despite steps that the government of Peru has taken to address labor conditions, union and NGO officials we met with reported that enforcement of labor laws remains weak and labor conditions have not improved in certain respects. According to State, Peru's labor laws place a 5-year limit on the continuous renewal of short-term labor contracts not leading to permanent employment in most sectors of the economy. However, State's 2013 Human Rights Report notes that a sector-specific law covering nontraditional export sectors such as apparel exempts employers from this 5-year limit and allows them to hire workers through indefinite series of short-term contracts. Union officials we met during our fieldwork also reported poor labor conditions in Peru's nontraditional export sectors, which these officials described as not affording the same labor rights as other sectors in the economy.[40] More generally, according to NGO officials, Peru's large informal sector makes it difficult for the government to enforce labor rights, because informal companies, which are not registered with the government and therefore are not subject to labor inspections, typically do not follow labor laws.

State's 2013 Human Rights Report also identifies continuing labor concerns in Peru's nontraditional export sectors, such as the effect of the use of temporary service contracts and subcontracting on workers' freedom of association. State's report also notes that in 2013, penalties for violations of freedom of association and collective bargaining were rarely enforced, the judicial process was prolonged, and employers were seldom penalized for dismissing workers involved in trade union activities. In addition, union officials whom we met with stated that Peru's agricultural law allows for workers to be paid less than the legal minimum wage and to be continuously hired on temporary contracts for 2- to 3- month periods. These officials stated that this limits workers' ability to collectively bargain and exercise freedom of association, because of fear that if they join a union, their contracts will not be renewed.

ONE OF FIVE LABOR SUBMISSIONS HAS BEEN RESOLVED, BUT REPORTING DEADLINES AND LIMITED PUBLIC AWARENESS OF THE PROCESS PRESENT PROBLEMS

DOL has accepted five of six labor submissions—that is, formal complaints alleging that FTA labor provisions had been violated—that it has received since 2008[41] and has closed one submission as resolved. However, DOL did not meet its original deadlines for reviewing and reporting on any of the submissions, exceeding the established 6-month submission review time frame by an average of about nine months and possibly delaying resolution of the submissions. Stakeholders whom we interviewed in the selected five partner countries generally expressed a lack of awareness or understanding of DOL's submission process, which may have limited the number of submissions filed. Moreover, stakeholders we interviewed expressed concerns about delays in resolving labor concerns detailed in the submissions for Guatemala and Honduras.

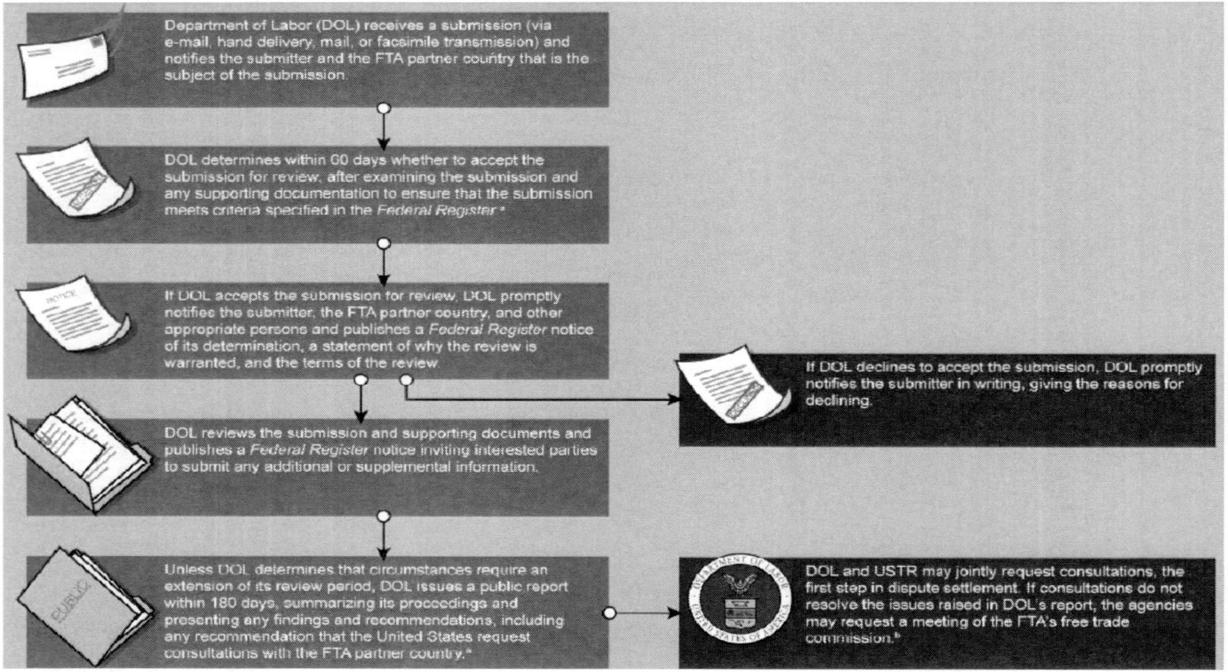

Source: GAO analysis of 71 Fed. Reg. 76791. | GAO-15-160.

Legend: FTA = free trade agreement, USTR = Office of the U.S. Trade Representative.

[a]DOL may extend the timeframe if it determines that circumstances require such an extension.

[b]The free trade commission established for each FTA is the primary forum for bilateral dialogue about the FTA's implementation.

Figure 2. U.S. DOL Labor Submission Process.

DOL Announced Its Process for Receiving and Evaluating Submissions in 2006

According to DOL, FTA labor provisions establish official processes for receiving submissions from interested organizations that believe a trading partner is not fulfilling its labor commitments. In the United States, DOL generally receives and reviews submissions made under the labor chapters of each trade agreement. DOL issued procedural guidelines pertaining to this function via publication of a *Federal Register* notice in 2006.[42] The guidelines contain deadlines and substantive criteria for acceptance and investigation of submissions. For example, DOL shall determine whether to accept a submission within 60 days and is to consider, among other things, whether it contains statements that, if substantiated, would constitute a failure by the other party to comply with its commitments under an FTA. If DOL determines that the circumstances require, the 60-day timeframe can be extended. According to DOL, its decision to review a public submission does not indicate any determination as to the validity or accuracy of the allegations contained in the submission; the submission's merit is addressed in the public report that follows DOL's review and analysis. DOL officials noted that although DOL has responsibility for investigating submissions, USTR, DOL, and State work together to engage diplomatically to address concerns.

Figure 2 illustrates DOL's submission process, including the established time frames for accepting and reviewing submissions.

DOL Has Closed One of Five Labor Submissions Accepted since 2008

Since 2008, DOL has accepted labor submissions filed under the Bahrain, Dominican Republic, Guatemala, Honduras, and Peru FTAs and has closed the Peru FTA submission.[43] The submissions for Bahrain, the Dominican Republic, and Guatemala—accepted in 2011, 2012, and 2008, respectively—remain open while the U.S. government engages with the governments to address the concerns that the submissions raised. The submission for Honduras, accepted in 2012, remains open while DOL reviews its allegations. Figure 3 presents information about the five submissions (see app. III for further details).

Bahrain	2011	• Violation of right to freedom of association • Discrimination	Open	U.S. government held second-round consultations with Bahraini government on June 22-23, 2014.
Dominican Republic	2012	• Human trafficking • Forced labor • Retaliatory firing of workers for union activities	Open	U.S. government is engaging with Dominican Republic government.
Guatemala	2008	• Violation of right to freedom of association • Violation of rights to organize and bargain collectively • Unacceptable work conditions	Open	U.S. and Guatemalan governments signed an Enforcement Plan in April 2013, addressing concerns raised in the submission. U.S. government granted Guatemalan government a 4-month extension in April 2014 to continue implementing the plan and granted a further 4-week extension in August 2014. U.S. government determined in September 2014 to proceed with dispute settlement, because Guatemala had not met the Enforcement Plan's terms.
Honduras	2012	• Violation of right to freedom of association • Violations of rights to organize and bargain collectively • Child labor	Open	U.S. government engagement is pending DOL's submission reviews.
Peru	2011	• Failure to comply with labor laws related to collective bargaining	Closed as resolved (2012)	

Source: GAO analysis of Department of Labor (DOL) information. | GAO-15-160.

Notes: DOL has also accepted other labor submissions under the North American Agreement on Labor Cooperation, which we did not examine.

Alleged violations shown for the Bahrain, Dominican Republic, Guatemala, and Honduras submissions are examples of those detailed in the submissions.

Figure 3. Free Trade Agreement (FTA) Labor Submissions Accepted by DOL as of July 2014.

DOL Did Not Meet 6- Month Time Frame for Any Submission, Showing the Time Frame to Be Unrealistic

Although DOL accepted most of the submissions it received within the 60- day time frame established by its guidelines, it did not complete its reviews of the submission within the established 180-day time frame.[44] A DOL official we met with indicated that DOL cannot complete within the 180-

day time frame the types of comprehensive investigations and reports it has been providing.

For each of the submissions, DOL determined at the end of the original 180-day review time frame to extend the review period and reported its findings and recommendations an average of 262 days after the original time frame had ended. According to USTR and DOL, before DOL publishes its review of a submission, both agencies engage informally with the relevant partner country to explore ways to address the concerns raised in the submission. However, USTR and DOL do not request formal consultations with a partner country to address DOL's recommendations until DOL has issued its report. As a result, extensions of DOL's review time frame may delay resolution of the submission.

- **Bahrain**. DOL received the Bahrain submission on April 21, 2011, and accepted it on June 10, 2011, or 50 days later. In December 2011, DOL extended the submission review period to consider and review additional information received from the government of Bahrain and Bahraini workers, amendments made to the Bahraini Trade Union Law, and labor-related developments in international forums. DOL issued its report on December 20, 2012, 559 days after accepting the submission.
- **Dominican Republic**. DOL received the Dominican Republic submission on December 22, 2011, and accepted it on February 22, 2012, or 62 days later. In August 2012, DOL extended the review time frame to consider public comments about the submission as well as information gathered by a Bureau of International Labor Affairs delegation during a visit to the Dominican Republic. DOL issued its report on September 27, 2013, 583 days after accepting the submission.
- **Guatemala**. DOL received the Guatemala submission on April 23, 2008, and accepted it on June 12, 2008, or 50 days later. DOL issued its report on January 16, 2009, 218 days after accepting the Guatemala submission.
- **Honduras**. DOL received the submission on March 26, 2012, and accepted it on May 14, 2012, or 49 days later. On November 2, 2012, 5 days before DOL's 180-day reporting deadline, DOL extended its review because of the scope of the submission, the scope of the alleged labor law violations, and the large amounts of information received from the Honduran government and stakeholders. As of

September 2014, DOL officials were continuing to review documentation of the allegations and prepare their report. DOL officials were unable to estimate when they would issue a public report.

- **Peru**. DOL received the submission for Peru on December 29, 2010, and accepted it on July 19, 2011, or 202 days later. On January 20, 2012, 185 days after accepting the submission, DOL concluded that circumstances required an extension of time for a thorough and detailed review of the Peru submission. DOL issued its report for the Peru submission on August 30, 2012, 408 days after accepting it.

Although DOL has periodically reviewed and updated the submission process since establishing it in 1994, DOL officials told us that they have not reviewed or adjusted the submission review time frame to reflect the time it takes DOL to issue its reports after accepting the submissions. DOL's extensions of each submission review period since 2008 have shown this time frame to be unrealistic. Federal standards for internal control call on agency management to monitor and assess the effectiveness and efficiency of their operations over time and to promptly resolve any deficiencies.[45]

Interviewed Stakeholders Generally Did Not Understand the Labor Submission Process, and U.S. Agencies Have Made Minimal Efforts to Explain It

Our interviews with union and other nongovernmental stakeholders in the selected partner countries suggested that little or no awareness and understanding of the FTA labor submission process may have affected the number of submissions filed. Union representatives we interviewed in our five case study countries—Colombia, El Salvador, Guatemala, Oman, and Peru—were generally either unaware of DOL's labor submission process or considered it difficult to understand and use. For example, a union representative in Colombia stated that the union would have filed a submission if the representative had known about the process. In another example, representatives of one of the larger El Salvador unions— GMIES, an NGO that monitors the actions of the Salvadorian government—stated that it was difficult for a "typical worker" to file a submission with DOL and that the information required for the submission is generally difficult, if not impossible, to obtain and document. A small number of union representatives who were aware of the process attributed their knowledge to information received from AFL-CIO or their country's Solidarity Center.[46] For instance, in Guatemala, a representative of a union that had signed the current Guatemala submission stated that without the help of the Solidarity Center, the union would have been unable to locate submission instructions and file the submission.

Moreover, although the government officials we interviewed in the five countries knew of the labor submission process, only in El Salvador did these officials express an understanding of how DOL evaluates a submission and conducts its fact-finding investigations. For example, the Guatemalan Ministry of Labor officials we interviewed could not provide information about how the process works or describe the criteria DOL uses to evaluate a submission's merits. The Ministry of Manpower officials whom we interviewed in Oman did not understand the purpose of the submission process or how submissions could be filed.

In addition, U.S. agencies have made minimal efforts to publicize the process for nongovernment stakeholders, who are most likely to file submissions. Federal standards for internal control pertaining to information and communication call for agencies to have relevant, reliable, and timely communications relating to internal as well as external events, to ensure control of their operations.[47] According to DOL officials, DOL relies exclusively on its website and its 2006 *Federal Register* notice to inform the public about the process.[48] Moreover, U.S. officials whom we interviewed in the countries we visited indicated that they do not advertise the existence of the submission process. Without additional efforts to inform nongovernment stakeholders in FTA partner countries about the DOL labor submission process, U.S. agencies are limited in their ability to use the submission process as a means of holding FTA partners accountable for fulfilling their labor commitments.

Some Stakeholders Expressed Concern About Delays in Resolving Labor Submissions

Several stakeholders we spoke with expressed concerns about delays in U.S. agencies' efforts to resolve the matters raised in the Guatemala and Honduras submissions. Because of the complexity of these matters, resolving them has proven difficult and time-consuming, according to USTR. Moreover, according to USTR, no process or time frames for U.S. agencies' efforts to engage diplomatically with FTA partners to resolve labor matters related to DOL submission reports are outlined in any active FTA that had entered into force or in U.S. implementing guidance.

According to USTR and DOL, they engage with FTA partners through informal and formal communication to resolve any FTA concerns. For example, according to a USTR official, USTR has informally engaged with FTA partners—through labor affairs council discussions, telephone conversations, and e-mail exchanges—for an average of 6 months regarding concerns raised in a submission before requesting formal consultations with the partner government.[49] If an FTA partner does not address USTR's and DOL's labor concerns or is unwilling to informally engage, USTR and DOL may request formal consultations under the FTA's labor chapter. USTR officials stated that an FTA partner's willingness to engage determines in part how quickly potential labor violations are addressed. According to USTR officials, some FTA partners are willing to engage informally to resolve labor violations, while other partners engage only after USTR and DOL have jointly requested formal consultations under the FTA's labor chapter.

Examples of stakeholders' concerns include the following.

- AFL-CIO representatives in Washington, D.C., who were involved with the Honduras and Guatemala submissions expressed appreciation of DOL's care in investigating cases and were eager to provide requisite evidence. However, they expressed disappointment that both cases have taken longer than they anticipated, stating that justice delayed can mean justice denied when workers' livelihoods are at stake.
- A union representative in Guatemala expressed disappointment that 6 years after the submission was filed, it had not been resolved. He also said that the steps outlined in the enforcement plan were mainly administrative and did not address all complaints detailed in the submission. As a result, according to the union representative, the conditions of workers identified in the submission have not improved.
- Four government officials from CAFTA-DR partner countries whom we interviewed in Washington, D.C., described DOL's submission process as lacking fairness and transparency. According to these representatives, DOL does not give partner governments clear information about next steps or access to evidence supporting the submissions and deprives the countries of the opportunity to respond to allegations presented by any member of the public.[50] The CAFTA-

DR representatives added that in their opinion, DOL conducts the submission process in an adversarial manner and that the process therefore does not function as a mechanism for addressing concerns on a cooperative basis. The representatives noted that this, in turn, can delay or complicate resolution of problems.

U.S. AGENCIES PROVIDE LIMITED MONITORING, ENFORCEMENT, AND REPORTING ON FTA LABOR PROVISIONS

Since 2009, USTR and DOL, with State's assistance, have taken steps intended to strengthen monitoring and enforcement of FTA partners' compliance with FTA labor provisions, but their monitoring and enforcement remain limited.[51]

After USTR announced in July 2009 that the agencies would take a more proactive, interagency approach to monitoring and enforcing FTA labor provisions, USTR and DOL developed mechanisms to track labor conditions and practices in priority trade partner countries. They also took some proactive monitoring steps with several FTA partners. However, although they jointly address labor submissions and work together to engage with partner countries regarding labor concerns, USTR and DOL have not established a coordinated strategic approach to systematically assess and address other possible inconsistencies with the FTA labor provisions, such as concerns that DOL identifies in internal management reports. The lack of such an approach may be inconsistent with USTR's 2009 announcement as well as with best practices for interagency collaboration. Agency officials cited limited funding and staffing as constraints on their ability to monitor and enforce FTA labor provisions.

USTR's, DOL's, and State's annual reports to Congress provide information about labor conditions in partner countries. However, reflecting in part USTR's and DOL's limited monitoring and enforcement of FTA labor provisions, the reports generally do not detail concerns about the implementation of FTA labor provisions by partner countries that have not been the subject of labor submissions. .

USTR and DOL Pledged in 2009 to Strengthen Monitoring and Enforcement of FTA Labor Provisions

In 2009, USTR made a public statement pledging to address weaknesses in monitoring and enforcement of FTA labor provisions such as those we identified in our July 2009 report.[52] In its statement, USTR—which has principal responsibility for monitoring and enforcing statutory trade agreements—publicly announced its intention to adopt a proactive, interagency approach to monitoring and enforcing FTA labor provisions in cooperation with DOL and State.[53] According to USTR's announcement, for example, the agencies would no longer enforce labor obligations only in response to complaints, would hold trading partners to their obligations on labor standards, and would work in close partnership to immediately identify and investigate labor violations. In addition, USTR's July 2009 announcement stated that the agencies would deploy resources more effectively to identify and solve problems at the source and would jointly engage with governments of countries that violate the rules, to quickly restore workers' rights, assist partner countries to find a way to fix identified labor problems, and pursue legal remedies when other options are closed.

A broad range of activities underpins federal monitoring and enforcement efforts. For the purposes of this report, "monitoring" refers to federal activities that are undertaken to identify instances where foreign laws, regulations, and practices may be inconsistent with trade agreement provisions; "enforcement" refers to actions taken by USTR to secure foreign compliance with trade agreements, which can include initiating dispute settlement procedures that certain trade agreements provide. 54 When agencies identify possible inconsistencies with FTA provisions, agencies take a variety of actions to encourage and obtain foreign compliance with trade agreements. As we previously reported, according to records and staff at USTR and other agencies, monitoring and enforcement of trade agreements typically involves several key steps: identifying compliance problems, setting priorities, gathering and analyzing information, developing and implementing responses, taking actions to enforce agreements, and coordinating with other agencies.[55] Systematic implementation of these key steps is necessary to ensure that the agencies effectively and efficiently accomplish their objective and help ensure that management's directives are carried out.

In our July 2009 report, we found that U.S. agencies had not proactively monitored FTA partners' compliance with labor commitments and did not consider that they were required to do so. [56] Moreover, U.S. interaction with partners regarding labor issues after FTAs entered into force had been limited, usually in part because of the low priority attached to this function. Further, we found that U.S. agencies generally gave attention to problematic labor situations in certain FTA partners' export sectors only after media exposure of the situations.

USTR and DOL Track Partner Countries' Labor Conditions but Do Not Systematically Monitor and Enforce Compliance with FTA Labor Provisions

Since July 2009, USTR and DOL have taken steps intended to strengthen monitoring and enforcement of FTA partners' compliance with FTA labor provisions.[57] USTR staff indicated that an important component of USTR's and DOL's work occurs between an FTA's finalization and its entry into force. For example, for the Colombia FTA, the agencies worked with the Colombian government to establish the Labor Action Plan, outlining steps that the government was required to take before the FTA could receive congressional approval. (See app. III for information about the agencies' efforts to monitor Colombia's implementation of the Labor Action Plan).[58] In addition, DOL and other U.S. agencies have supported cooperative activities to assist the countries to be better positioned to meet their labor commitments after FTAs have entered into force.[59] In general, after FTAs have entered into force, USTR and DOL have engaged in discussions with partner countries, gathering information about labor conditions in the countries and responding to FTA labor concerns. In doing so, the agencies have addressed some of the typical key elements of monitoring and enforcement that we previously identified, such as gathering and analyzing information and setting priorities. However, the agencies' approach for countries other than Jordan, Panama, and, to some extent, Colombia and Peru generally does not incorporate other key elements, such as identifying compliance problems, developing and implementing responses, and taking enforcement actions.

USTR

In October 2012, USTR established the Trade Policy Staff Committee (TPSC) Subcommittee on Labor Monitoring and Enforcement to focus on monitoring and enforcing labor provisions in partner countries, with members from various agencies, including DOL and State.[60] USTR charged the subcommittee with monitoring and enforcing labor issues in 20 FTA partner countries as well as 146 countries that participate in U.S. trade preference programs. According to a USTR document, the subcommittee participates in efforts to enforce labor obligations, such as through submission reviews, consultation, and dispute settlement under FTAs.[61] However, according to DOL and State staff who have participated in the Subcommittee on Labor Monitoring and Enforcement, the subcommittee's meetings generally serve as an information-sharing mechanism rather than a monitoring and enforcement mechanism.[62] State participants described the subcommittee as an interagency process for reviewing and discussing labor conditions and assessing risks in trade partner countries, including FTA and trade preference program partners. State added that although this process does not entail a regular, detailed review of each FTA partner country's compliance with labor obligations, it facilitates discussion of concerns and development of next steps to address these concerns based on input from each agency. A USTR official stated that when the subcommittee met in October 2012 and February 2013, it decided that an emphasis on overseeing labor conditions in parts of Africa and Haiti was needed and that monitoring of FTA labor provisions' implementation would be based mainly on addressing DOL labor submissions. USTR officials noted that information sharing is a key part of its process to assess labor conditions in FTA partner countries relative to their commitments and to identify matters that are appropriate for further action.

According to a USTR official, work by the subcommittee and ad hoc interagency country teams has led to increased actions and engagement in countries such as Jordan, Panama, Peru, and Morocco, where, according to USTR, it has conducted, or expects to conduct, high-level labor meetings and monitoring trips in 2014. Further, according to USTR officials, USTR has used input from the subcommittee to develop a matrix to more comprehensively track monitoring activities and technical capacity-building assistance across FTA partner countries. USTR officials indicated that this tool has served as a point of departure for soliciting the subcommittee's input on priorities and coordination of future activities. In addition, according to USTR officials, USTR regularly coordinates and communicates with other agencies, industry, labor unions, the ILO and other external stakeholders to identify possible inconsistencies with the labor provisions of trade agreements.

USTR officials said that the agencies routinely address labor issues identified in the subcommittee or by other stakeholders through bilateral consultations and formally established FTA mechanisms, such as the labor affairs councils established by most FTAs and the FTA free trade commissions, which are the main forums for bilateral dialogue about FTA implementation for each FTA. USTR has publicly reported on such meetings, as we recommended in 2009. However, the labor affairs councils for most FTAs have in most cases met only once and in two cases have not met at all since the FTAs entered into force.[63] Moreover, the FTA free trade commissions' discussions reportedly do not address labor issues in depth. For example, officials from the Ministry of Labor in Peru indicated that in the last free trade commission meeting they attended, labor issues were not substantively addressed; instead members of the commission agreed that a meeting on the topic could be held later in the year.

USTR officials stated that monitoring and enforcement covers a large spectrum of activities and that in some cases USTR has taken steps to resolve issues in countries where submissions have not been filed. For example, according to USTR officials, USTR and DOL negotiated an implementation plan in 2012 to address concerns regarding foreign workers in Jordan's garment sector and have continued to monitor Jordan's implementation of its FTA labor commitments. USTR officials also cited as examples of proactive monitoring and enforcement USTR's engagement with Colombia regarding the Action Plan, cooperation with Panama in passing administrative and legal changes to address labor concerns as part of the FTA ratification process in 2011, and discussions with Peru regarding commitments that the government made in 2007 to improve respect of labor rights for temporary and subcontracted workers.

Our analysis shows that in Jordan and Panama, USTR's and DOL's activities have addressed the typical key elements of monitoring and enforcement. Regarding Jordan, USTR documents indicate that USTR and DOL have addressed all key elements of monitoring and enforcement, such as by putting in place a concrete plan to fix an identified problem and taking steps to assure that the plan is implemented. Regarding Panama, USTR documents show that the agencies took steps to assure that Panama met its commitments both before and after the FTA entered into effect in 2012 and have been pursuing steps, such as holding several recent meetings, that may help in resolving outstanding concerns about implementation of FTA labor provisions.

However, while USTR's and DOL's reported monitoring activities in Colombia and Peru can assist the countries to be better positioned to meet their FTA labor commitments and help to better inform USTR of labor concerns in these countries, the evidence that we examined does not demonstrate systematic implementation of the typical key elements for monitoring and enforcement of labor provisions.

- **Colombia.** Documentation that USTR and DOL provided, as well as evidence that we gathered in Colombia and in interviews with agency officials, indicates that the agencies took several of the key steps of monitoring and enforcement. For example, a report that USTR and DOL jointly prepared in 2014 showed that the agencies have been gathering and analyzing information, setting priorities, assessing implementation, and identifying compliance problems. However, we did not see evidence that a current plan is in place to address the outstanding concerns that USTR and DOL have identified.
- **Peru.** Documentation that USTR and DOL provided demonstrates a systematic approach to some, but not all, of the monitoring and enforcement steps that we identified. Specifically, both agencies have engaged to some extent with Peru regarding labor matters in the 5 years since the Peru FTA went into effect. The agencies' documentation shows that at least some of their efforts to gather and analyze information regarding Peru relate to verifying the government's implementation and enforcement of previous reforms, such as reforms of its labor inspection regime and of its legal framework for temporary employment and subcontracting. USTR and DOL documents also show that the agencies have identified several possible compliance concerns and have engaged with the government by scheduling meetings and asking questions. However, we did not see evidence of a plan to resolve outstanding U.S. concerns. Further, in July 2014, Peru announced that it had enacted legal changes that rolled back previously implemented improvements in its labor laws in areas such as health and safety protection for workers, to improve the business climate and attract investment.

DOL

To strengthen its monitoring and enforcement of FTA labor provisions, in 2012, DOL established the Monitoring and Enforcement of Trade Agreements Division within the Bureau of International Labor Affairs' Office of Trade and Labor Affairs.[64] The division's objectives are to ensure that partner governments (1) effectively enforce their labor laws and implement policies that protect worker rights; (2) understand their commitments under the FTA labor chapters; and (3) revise or adopt laws, regulations, and policies consistent with international labor standards. The division mainly monitors implementation of FTA labor provisions through its review of FTA labor submissions and through the use of internal documents called management reports, according to DOL officials.[65] However, DOL uses management reports to identify labor concerns rather than to fully assess consistency with FTA labor provisions.

- **FTA labor submissions.** DOL's review of the five FTA labor submissions—for Bahrain, the Dominican Republic, Guatemala, Honduras, and Peru—that it has accepted since 2008 have led to recommendations in three of its submission reports that the partners address alleged violations of FTA labor provisions. [66] According to USTR officials, labor submissions are a central component of the FTAs' framework for monitoring and enforcement of labor obligations and USTR and DOL invest extensive time and resources in addressing submissions. For the Bahrain and Guatemala submissions, DOL, with USTR, formally requested labor consultations under the FTAs' labor chapters to address the concerns raised in the submissions. In Guatemala's case, after consultations failed to address the concerns, the U.S. government invoked dispute settlement proceedings; during these proceedings, the two governments negotiated the Enforcement Plan, outlining steps that Guatemala agreed to take. (See app. III for a discussion of DOL's monitoring of Guatemala's implementation of the Enforcement Plan.)
- **Internal management reports.** In 2012, according to DOL staff, DOL began consistently monitoring FTA-related labor issues in 13 FTA partner countries. The management reports provide, among other information, a synopsis of labor conditions in partner countries based on sources such as State, ILO, the International Trade Union Confederation, local stakeholders, and the press. The reports include updated contact information for each partner and identify labor conditions or practices—for example, related to freedom of association and collective bargaining—that may be inconsistent with the FTA labor provisions. They also outline steps that DOL staff propose to take to address any identified concerns, subject to approval and resource availability. According to DOL officials, DOL uses the management reports to identify labor concerns, rather than potential FTA violations for enforcement purposes, and to facilitate engagement on technical assistance projects with FTA partner countries. DOL officials noted that claiming and proving a violation of FTA labor provisions would be very costly and legally complicated. The officials explained that when a management report

identifies labor concerns, DOL may request formal or informal consultations with the partner country's ministry of labor to discuss these concerns and will attempt to cooperatively address them. The officials also noted that a persistent condition may result in a submission from a stakeholder.

USTR and DOL Lack a Coordinated Strategic Approach to Address Identified Labor Issues

USTR and DOL work together on an ad hoc basis to address labor concerns identified in submissions and to engage with partner countries regarding labor matters. However, the agencies have not developed a coordinated strategic approach to systematically assess and address other possible inconsistencies with FTA labor provisions, such as the issues that DOL's management reports identify, in other partner countries. This lack of a joint approach may be inconsistent with USTR's 2009 statement that the agencies would work in close partnership to immediately identify and investigate labor violations.

Further, while the agencies take steps such as gathering facts from credible and reliable sources and prioritizing their monitoring of the partner countries, they have not jointly operationalized other key steps that we previously identified as typical for monitoring and enforcement of trade agreements. For example, although DOL's management reports are its primary means, other than submissions, of monitoring and identifying issues that may be inconsistent with FTA labor provisions, the agencies have not established a coordinated strategic approach to identify and carry out steps necessary to address issues identified in the reports. According to DOL, the management reports are available to USTR and State and the three agencies routinely discuss the reports' contents. USTR confirmed that DOL shares information from the reports with the Subcommittee on Labor Monitoring and Enforcement for discussion and consideration. However, USTR officials noted that USTR regards the management reports as one of multiple information sources that it considers before deciding to engage with a country about a labor concern, rather than as an indicator of a need to engage with the country. USTR officials also noted that USTR views the management reports as a new internal DOL tool and is assessing how best to use these reports in the interagency process.

Moreover, USTR, DOL, and State have differing perspectives on how to monitor and enforce FTA labor provisions, according to agency officials. According to a USTR official, each agency approaches monitoring and enforcement in relation to its mission, and as a result, some of the 13 countries that DOL has identified internally as priorities differ from countries that USTR has identified as priorities in the context of the FTAs. The USTR official stated that USTR must assess whether a labor issue constitutes a breach of obligations set forth in the relevant FTA before it pursues dispute settlement, whereas DOL and State—as observers of labor conditions and human rights, respectively—approach labor issues more strictly as labor rights concerns. According to a State official, USTR prefers to address identified partner countries' labor issues without the intent to invoke the FTA.

Our prior work identifying best practices for interagency collaboration has shown that agencies can enhance and sustain their collaborative efforts by engaging in eight practices.[67] For example, to achieve a common outcome, collaborating agencies need to, among other things, not only define and articulate the outcome but also establish strategies that work in concert with their partners' or are joint in nature. Such strategies help in aligning the partner agencies' activities, core processes, and resources to accomplish the common outcome.

U.S. Agencies Focus Limited Monitoring and Enforcement Resources on a Few Priority Countries

Agency officials cited limited staffing and resources as constraints on their ability to proactively monitor and enforce implementation of FTA labor provisions as the number of FTAs increases, leading the agencies to focus most of their efforts in a few priority countries. The agencies described enforcement activities as particularly resource intensive. DOL officials told us that because they had to focus much of their available resources on enforcing the Colombia Labor Action Plan and the Guatemala Enforcement Plan, their ability to monitor and enforce FTA partners' compliance with their FTAs' labor provisions in the last year was limited. Given the staffing and resource constraints that USTR, DOL, and State officials cited, effective interagency collaboration—including joint strategies that assist in aligning partner agencies' activities, core processes, and resources to more effectively accomplish the common outcome—is essential to maximize the agencies' ability to monitor and enforce compliance with these provisions.[68]

USTR

Staffing and funding constraints have, at times, limited the office's engagement with FTA partner countries regarding labor matters, according to USTR officials. Notably, according to the officials, recent sequestration-related cuts at USTR sharply limited travel. The officials told us that USTR's Office of Labor Affairs has four staff members—an Assistant U.S. Trade Representative for Labor, two Deputy Assistant U.S. Trade Representatives for Labor, and the Director for Labor Affairs— whose responsibilities include, among others, negotiating labor provisions in new agreements such as the Trans-Pacific Partnership, overseeing labor matters for 20 FTA partner countries and 120 trade preference countries, and engaging with countries to address labor complaints. According to USTR officials, although the Office of Labor Affairs staff has doubled from two to four since 2008, the number of trade partner countries for which they are responsible has increased from 14 to 20. USTR staff stated that because so few staff are available, they cannot engage with partner countries regarding every labor issue identified and must address such issues in cooperation with other agencies. USTR staff also noted that they depend on DOL and State for day-to-day monitoring of labor conditions in partner countries.

DOL

Resource constraints limit DOL's ability to monitor implementation of FTA labor provisions except in partner countries that DOL has identified as priorities, such as countries cited in labor submissions, according to DOL officials. DOL reported that in fiscal years 2013 and 2014, the Monitoring and Enforcement of Trade Agreements Division had five to eight full-time staff, with primary responsibilities that include monitoring labor conditions in 20 FTA partners and addressing and following up on labor submissions—for example, assessing implementation of submission report recommendations and engaging in consultations with the FTA partner. DOL officials stated that over the past year, the division's staff spent 80 percent of their work hours monitoring implementation of the Guatemala Enforcement Plan; following up on activities initiated under the Colombia Labor Action Plan; and addressing labor submissions for Honduras, the Dominican Republic, Bahrain, and Mexico.[69] The employees' remaining work hours were available to monitor and engage with the other 14 FTA partner countries. DOL officials expressed concern that challenges related to resource limitations will grow as the number of FTAs increases. For example, according to DOL and State officials,

Vietnam is among the countries participating in the Trans-Pacific Partnership negotiations with a poor record of protecting labor rights.

State

State has limited resources available to support USTR's and DOL's monitoring of FTA labor provisions, according to State officials. State's Bureau of Democracy, Human Rights, and Labor (DRL) coordinates State's in-country labor officers or labor reporting officers, who carry out regular monitoring and reporting and day-to-day interaction with foreign governments on labor matters. However, these staff are not responsible for monitoring implementation of labor provisions in the FTAs. State informs USTR and DOL about labor concerns identified in FTA partner countries, through reporting cables and other means, and supports them in investigating labor submissions and addressing related recommendations. DRL has seven staff at State's headquarters in Washington, D.C., one of whom focuses on trade-related issues, who are supported by labor affairs officers and labor reporting officers at the embassies in each of the 20 FTA partner countries.[70] State officials explained that each of these labor affairs officers and labor reporting officers has other responsibilities. Overall, the amount of time that these officers dedicated to labor issues varied from 5 percent (in Australia) to 75 percent (in Mexico).

U.S. Agencies' Annual Reports Address FTA Partners' Labor Conditions to an Extent

USTR, DOL, and State provide required annual reports to Congress that contain some information about labor conditions in FTA partner countries. However, the annual reports generally do not detail concerns about the implementation of FTA labor provisions by partner countries that have not been the subject of labor submissions, in part reflecting the agencies' limited monitoring and enforcement of the provisions.[71] USTR has statutory responsibility to report to Congress about trade agreement programs on an annual basis. According to DOL and State, they do not have such a responsibility, although some of their required reports include related information.

USTR

Each year, USTR provides Congress with the current Trade Policy Agenda for the current year, as well as the *Annual Report of the President of the United States on the Trade Agreement Programs*. The agenda and the annual report include information about trade policy priorities and actions taken to implement FTAs. For example, the 2014 agenda indicates, among other things, that USTR will seek to ensure that trade partners meet their obligations related to labor rights, will focus on implementation of FTAs, and will work with key partner countries to address specific labor issues. The 2013 annual report describes, among other things, the status of the labor submissions regarding Bahrain, Guatemala, the Dominican Republic, and Honduras and USTR's efforts to address the concerns that the submissions identify; in some cases, possible inconsistencies with the FTA may be discussed. However, the annual report generally does not detail concerns about the implementation of FTA labor provisions by partner countries that have not been the subject of labor submissions, reflecting in part USTR's and DOL's limited monitoring and enforcement of these provisions. Including appropriate information resulting from more extensive monitoring and enforcement could help inform Congress and other U.S. stakeholders about the extent to which trade partners are fulfilling their FTA labor commitments.

DOL

DOL is required to report to Congress every 2 years regarding labor issues related to CAFTA-DR but is not required to report on the implementation of labor provisions in other FTAs. For CAFTA-DR, DOL is required to submit a biennial report to Congress on the progress made by the CAFTA-DR partner countries in implementing the labor chapter provisions and labor cooperation and capacity-building activities.[72] DOL's 2011 report on CAFTA-DR summarizes the progress made by each CAFTA-DR partner country in implementing these provisions and activities, although the report generally does not detail concerns about the implementation of CAFTA-DR labor provisions.

State

Every year, State provides Congress with the annual *Country Reports on Human Rights Practices*, which covers all countries receiving assistance and all United Nations member states, including all U.S. FTA partners. Each of the country reports includes a section on labor issues, covering topics such as internationally recognized individual, civil, political, and worker rights, as set forth in the Universal Declaration of Human Rights and other international agreements. In addition, most of the country reports for FTA partner countries that we reviewed include information about unfavorable conditions faced by workers and any challenges to the partner countries' implementation of their labor laws. The reports generally do not—and, according to State, are not intended to—detail concerns about the implementation of FTA labor provisions.

CONCLUSION

The United States' recent FTAs have served as means of securing commitments from trade partners to uphold and protect internationally recognized labor rights. Although the FTA partners we selected for our review have made some progress, with U.S. assistance, in implementing their FTA labor commitments, enforcement weaknesses and problematic labor conditions persist. In addition, nongovernment stakeholders we interviewed in partner countries had little or no awareness of the labor submission process that DOL established to allow such stakeholders to register concerns about FTA partners' labor practices. Further, DOL's extensions of its 6-month submission review time frame by an average of nine months per submission has shown the time frame to be unrealistic. Moreover, U.S. agencies' work with the partners to resolve these concerns has in some cases been very time consuming. For example, 6 years after DOL received the Guatemala labor submission, the submission remains open, and according to U.S. agencies, Guatemala has not fully addressed the weaknesses in its labor law enforcement or the resulting hardships on workers.

Further, although USTR and DOL jointly pledged in 2009 to adopt a more assertive, interagency approach to monitoring and enforcing FTA labor provisions, in practice the agencies systematically investigate possible inconsistencies with these provisions primarily in response to labor submissions. In addition, despite ongoing interaction between USTR and DOL—for example, in addressing submissions—they have not developed a strategic approach to jointly set priorities and coordinate efforts to respond to labor concerns such as those identified in the DOL management reports. Without such strategic coordination, and given constraints on resources, both agencies have focused their monitoring and enforcement activities, apart from addressing labor submissions, on a few priority countries. As a result, consistency with FTA labor provisions in most partner countries is generally not monitored and enforced systematically. Moreover, USTR may be limited in its ability to report to Congress regarding concerns about FTA partners' implementation of their respective FTA labor commitments.

RECOMMENDATIONS FOR EXECUTIVE ACTION

To improve the capacity of the U.S. government to monitor and enforce FTA partners' compliance with mutually agreed FTA labor provisions, we are making four recommendations to the U.S. Trade Representative and the Secretary of Labor.

- We recommend that DOL reevaluate and adjust, if necessary, its FTA labor submission review time frame to ensure that it more accurately reflects the time required to thoroughly investigate and to report on most labor submissions.
- We recommend that DOL take steps to better inform stakeholders in FTA partner countries about its FTA labor submission process.
- We recommend that USTR and DOL, in cooperation with State, establish a coordinated strategic approach to monitoring and enforcing FTA labor provisions, to ensure that they systematically assess the consistency of priority FTA partner countries' laws, regulations, and practices with trade agreement labor provisions and address any identified concerns.
- We recommend that USTR ensure that the *Annual Report of the President of the United States on the Trade Agreement Programs*, which USTR provides each year to Congress, includes results of USTR's and DOL's efforts to proactively monitor partner countries' compliance with FTA labor provisions.

AGENCY COMMENTS AND OUR EVALUATION

We provided a draft of our report to USTR, DOL, State, and USAID. USTR and DOL provided written comments. USTR, DOL, and State also provided extensive technical comments, which we incorporated or addressed as appropriate. USAID did not provide comments.

In their written comments, USTR and DOL expressed general agreement with our recommendations. USTR wrote that it embraced the recommendation to improve coordination with the Departments of Labor and State, to identify and address areas of concern, and to ensure that its reporting to Congress effectively reflects the results of these efforts. DOL committed to reevaluate its internal submission review process, in consultation with USTR and State, to determine whether internal adjustments may be necessary. DOL also said that it will evaluate additional available actions to expand its ability to inform stakeholders in FTA partner countries about the FTA labor submission process. Finally, DOL said that it will evaluate additional options to increase its proactive monitoring and enforcement of labor provisions in FTAs and its coordination with USTR and State on such issues.

Nevertheless, USTR and DOL took issue with our findings that the agencies do not systematically monitor and enforce labor provisions for all FTA partners and lack a coordinated strategic approach to monitoring and enforcement. Although we made some adjustments in response to new information that USTR and DOL provided with their comments, we maintain that, in general, the two agencies have not systematically implemented all key elements of monitoring and enforcement with regard to FTA labor provisions. We acknowledge that USTR, DOL, and State generally collaborate in engaging with partner countries on labor issues and in addressing submissions. However, the evidence that we reviewed, such as agendas for interagency meetings and our interviews with USTR and DOL staff, did not show that the agencies have developed a coordinated, strategic approach to systematically address possible inconsistencies with FTA labor provisions in most partner countries that have not been the subject of labor submissions. For example, we did not see evidence of a coordinated approach to address issues such as those identified by USTR in the partner countries it designates as high risk or that DOL identifies in its management reports.

Kimberly Gianopoulos
Acting Director, International Affairs & Trade

APPENDIX I: OBJECTIVES, SCOPE, AND METHODOLOGY

This report examines (1) steps that selected partner countries have taken, and U.S. assistance they have received, to implement free trade agreement (FTA) labor provisions and other labor initiatives and the reported results of such steps; (2) complaints—known as submissions— about possible violations of FTA labor provisions that DOL has accepted and any problems related to the submission process; and (3) the extent to which the Office of the U.S. Trade Representative (USTR), Department of Labor (DOL), and Department of State (State) monitor and enforce partner countries' implementation of FTA labor provisions and report results to Congress. In addition, appendix II describes reported violence against labor unionists in selected FTA partner countries as well as steps that the countries have taken to address such occurrences. Appendix III describes U.S. agencies' efforts to monitor implementation of other labor initiatives. Appendix IV describes the status of labor submissions received by the Department of Labor.

We chose to concentrate our review on four FTAs and five partners to these FTAs, so that we could examine the unique set of circumstances for FTA partner countries with some specificity. The FTAs and partner countries on which we chose to focus—the Dominican Republic-Central America-United States (CAFTA-DR), among whose six partner countries we selected El Salvador and Guatemala; the Colombia FTA; the Oman FTA; and the Peru FTA—are FTAs that contain labor provisions and countries with regional dispersion across Central America, South America, and the Middle East. We also selected CAFTA-DR because of the CAFTA-DR White Paper labor initiatives, and we selected El Salvador and Guatemala among CAFTA-DR countries because of the extent of U.S. assistance for labor programs and, in Guatemala's case, the FTArelated Enforcement Plan. In addition, we selected the Colombia FTA because of the Labor Action Plan, and we chose the Colombia and Peru FTAs because they contain language echoing the Bipartisan Trade Agreement of May 10, 2007, popularly known as the May 10th Agreement. However, the results of our review of these selected FTAs and partner countries cannot be generalized to all FTAs and partner countries.

In gathering information for each of our objectives, we engaged in three types of activities:

- We obtained information and perspectives from U.S. government, foreign government, nongovernmental organization (NGO), labor union, and private sector officials; stakeholders such as umbrella business associations; and experts.
- We obtained information and analysis from legal and secondary literature sources.
- We obtained information through visits to partner countries.

During our visits to Colombia, El Salvador, Guatemala, Oman, and Peru, we met with U.S. officials; foreign government officials responsible for the implementation of labor provisions of the FTAs and other labor initiatives; umbrella business groups, such as chambers of commerce; officials of international organizations such as the International Labour Organization (ILO), trade unions, NGOs, and other subject matter experts. Additionally, we visited Costa Rica to meet with ILO officials in their Central America regional office, in San Jose. The views expressed by these officials and organizations cannot be generalized to all officials or organizations knowledgeable about labor provisions in the selected FTAs.

Objective 1: Examine Steps That Selected Partner Countries Have Taken, and U.S. Assistance They Have Received, to Implement FTA Labor Provisions and Other Labor Initiatives and the Reported Results of Such Steps

To examine the steps that the selected FTA partner countries have taken to implement labor protection commitments under the respective agreements and other labor initiatives in the context of the respective FTAs, as well as the reported results of these steps, we obtained, reviewed, and analyzed documents from a variety of sources, including the four selected FTAs and their associated labor annexes as well as the CAFTA-DR White Paper and the Colombia Labor Action Plan. For this analysis, we included steps taken by partner countries, beginning with FTA negotiations for each FTA through May 2014. We also reviewed congressionally mandated reports, such as State's *Country Reports on Human Rights Practices* (Human Rights Reports), of which the 2013 reports were the latest available; USTR's annual trade agenda and trade report; and DOL's biennial *Progress in Implementing Chapter 16 (Labor) and Capacity Building under the Dominican Republic-Central America-United States Free Trade Agreement*. In addition, we reviewed reports submitted to Congress in conjunction with FTA implementing legislation, such as DOL's *Labor Rights Reports* for each of our selected FTAs.

Additionally, we interviewed officials from DOL's International Labor Affairs Bureau and the Office of Trade and Labor Affairs; USTR's Labor Affairs office; and State's Bureau of Democracy, Human Rights, and Labor. We also interviewed State desk officers responsible for selected partner countries and labor, political, and economic officers at U.S. embassies. In each of the selected countries, except Colombia, we interviewed officials from the relevant ministries, including the ministry of labor. (Colombia's Ministry of Labor chose to provide written responses to our questions.) We did not independently identify or evaluate FTA partner countries' enforcement or compliance with laws and procedures but rather relied on evidence obtained from U.S. and partner government as well as stakeholder sources. Because of the ILO's role in interpreting, assessing, and improving signatories' compliance with ILO Conventions and Fundamental Principles, we conducted a series of meetings at the ILO in Geneva as well as with umbrella organizations participating in the ILO's tripartite (government-business-labor) governance structure.

To examine U.S. funding for labor-related assistance projects, we collected data on such funding obligations—from the date when Congress passed the respective FTA implementing legislation through 2013—from relevant officials at State, DOL, and USAID and publicly available data on trade-related labor assistance from USAID's Trade Capacity Building Database. We assessed the reliability of the data by (1) interviewing agency officials knowledgeable about the data sources and (2) tracing the data to source documents. We determined that the data were sufficiently reliable for the purposes of describing U.S. assistance for labor provisions in FTA countries. In addition, to identify any changes in levels of reported violence against workers exercising labor rights in the selected countries and the partner governments' responses (see app. II), we obtained, reviewed, and analyzed documents from USTR, DOL, and State, such as State's Human Rights Reports and DOL's *Labor Rights Reports*. During our fieldwork in each selected country, we interviewed U.S. and foreign government officials, labor unions, and NGOs to learn of any violence against unionists. Of the countries we selected for review, violence against unionists was reported only in Colombia and Guatemala. During our fieldwork in Colombia, we interviewed and obtained information from entities responsible for collecting and reporting data on violence against unionists, including the Colombian Prosecutor General's office; ENS (Escuela Nacional Sindical)—a labor rights NGO—and State's Human Rights and Labor officers at the U.S. embassy in Bogota. We assessed the reliability of ENS's and the Colombian Prosecutor General's data by (1) interviewing officials from each entity about their criteria and data collection methodology for determining whether a victim's union activity was a motive in the killing and (2) interviewing State's Human Rights and Labor officers, who report ENS and Colombia's Prosecutor General's data in the annual Human Rights Report for Colombia. We determined the data to be sufficiently reliable for the purposes of describing reported violence against unionists in Colombia. In Guatemala, we interviewed, and obtained information from, the Guatemalan Prosecutor General's Office, which is responsible for prosecuting crimes against unionists, and the Guatemalan Ministry of the Interior, which investigates crimes against unionists at the direction of the Prosecutor General's Office. Because Guatemala did not collect data on violence against unionists, we did not review such data on homicide rates over time. We also interviewed State's political officer responsible for labor affairs at its embassy in Guatemala City, labor unions, and NGO officials. We reviewed ILO reports and discussed steps by Colombia and Guatemala to address violence with ILO officials. Our analysis was based on reputable secondary sources. We did not make any independent determination regarding the merit of any evidence of violence against unionists.

Objective 2: Examine Submissions about Possible Violations of FTA Labor Provisions That DOL Has Accepted and Any Problems Related to the Submission Process

To examine labor submissions that have been filed under FTA agreements and any problems related to the submission process, we obtained, reviewed, and analyzed documents, including each labor submission filed with DOL. We interviewed officials from DOL's Office of Trade and Labor Affairs—the office responsible for investigating and reporting on submissions—as well as USTR and State officials who review DOL's reports and are involved in following up with FTA partner countries, if needed. During our fieldwork, we interviewed union and NGO representatives involved in filing submissions, as well as relevant government ministries, including the Ministries of Labor in Peru and Guatemala.

Objective 3: Examine the Extent to Which USTR, DOL, and State Monitor and Enforce Partner Countries' Implementation of FTA Labor Provisions and Report Results to Congress

To examine the extent to which USTR, DOL, and State monitor and enforce implementation of FTA labor provisions and associated commitments (see app. III) and report results to Congress, we requested, reviewed, and analyzed documents from each agency. These documents included strategic plans and documents reflecting monitoring activities, such as DOL's management reports for 13 selected FTA partner countries, State cables, and USTR monitoring documents. In addition, we interviewed selected members of the USTR-chaired Trade Policy Staff Committee and its subcommittee on FTA labor monitoring and enforcement. To examine the resources that USTR, DOL, and State dedicate to monitoring labor provisions in FTAs, we obtained and analyzed data on staffing and other resources such as travel. We interviewed officials from DOL's International Labor Affairs Bureau and its Office of Trade and Labor Affairs; USTR; and State's Bureau of Democracy, Human Rights, and Labor, as well as State's in-country labor, labor reporting, political, and economic officers at U.S. embassies during our fieldwork. In addition, during our fieldwork, we interviewed officials from the partner countries' various ministries, including the ministries of labor, as well as representatives from labor unions and NGO officials implementing programs funded by U.S. agencies. To determine whether USTR, DOL, and State report the results of their monitoring activities to Congress, we reviewed and analyzed the agencies' reports, such as USTR's Trade Policy Agenda and Annual Report (2009 to 2013), DOL Annual Performance Reports (2010 to 2013), and State's Human Rights Reports (2009 to 2013). We conducted this performance audit work from May 2013 to November 2014 in accordance with generally accepted government auditing standards. Those standards require that we plan and perform the audit to obtain sufficient, appropriate evidence to provide a reasonable basis for our findings and conclusions based on our audit objectives. We believe that the evidence obtained provides a reasonable basis for our findings and conclusions based on our audit objectives.

Appendix II: Reported Violence against Trade Unionists in Colombia and Guatemala

Colombia

Violence and Threats of Violence against Unionists, Undermining Freedom of Association, Have Been Reported in Colombia

U.S. and Colombian officials and representatives of unions, nongovernmental organizations (NGO), and private sector groups we met with reported that violence against unionists continues to exist in Colombia, which union leaders and NGOs reported undermines workers' ability to freely associate because of the fear that their union activities may lead them to become victims of violence.[1] NGO officials in Colombia reported that although murders of unionists are a serious concern, threats of violence against union members also create a significant deterrent to workers organizing, with one NGO official noting a greater impact in rural areas than in major cities. According to this NGO official, authorities are less likely to have the capacity to investigate and respond to threats made in rural areas, with the result that victims flee the area or disengage from labor activities.

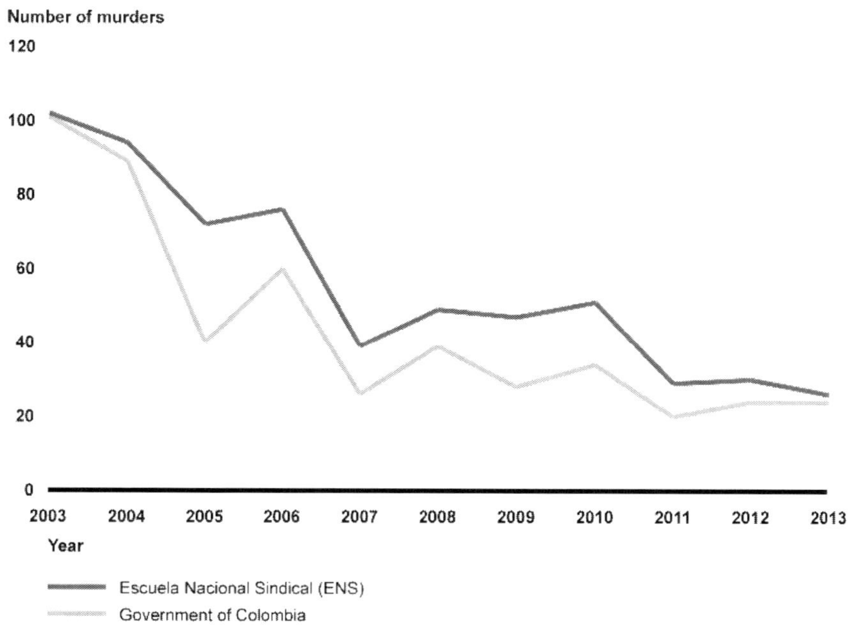

Source: GAO analysis of ENS and government of Columbia data, as reported by Department of State and Congressional Research Service. | GAO-15-160.

Figure 4. Murders of Unionists in Colombia, 2003-2013.

Data collected by the NGO Escuela Nacional Sindical (ENS) and the Colombia Prosecutor General's Office, as reported in the U.S. Department of State's Human Rights Reports, show that murders of trade unionists have generally decreased over the past decade, although homicides continue to occur (see fig. 4). [2] For example, according to DOL, as of July 2014 ENS had recorded 35 murders in 2013, compared with 102 murders of union members and labor activists in 2003. This trend continued in the period since the Labor Action Plan—which contains specific commitments to address labor violence—was announced in 2011. Labor union officials acknowledged the number of homicides has decreased, but they noted that violence continues to exist.

Further, according to ENS, as a result of the Labor Action Plan, ENS and the Prosecutor General's Office have developed a collaborative relationship, with the Prosecutor General's Office consulting with ENS on cases involving murders or threats that may be linked to the victims' union activities.

Government officials and labor groups we met with in Colombia all reported that threats of violence against unionists have been increasing. However, ENS is the only source of such threat data, and its reports do not show a clear pattern over the past decade.[3] ENS's data represent only reported threats; threats of violence against unionists may go unreported.

Colombia Has Taken Agreed Steps to Prevent and Investigate Violence against Trade Unionists, but Unions Report That Violence Persists

The government of Colombia committed to a number of reforms related to labor violence in April 2011 in the Labor Action Plan. Such commitments included broadening the scope of the government of Colombia's protection program, Unidad Nacional de Protección (UNP), to include labor activists, union members, and people engaging in efforts to form a union, increasing the budget for the additional resources necessary to support the expansion of the protection program, eliminating the backlog of protection applications awaiting risk assessments, completing future risk assessments within a 30-day period (as described below), and reforming the Colombian interagency committee that reviews risk assessments. In addition, Colombia committed to criminal justice reforms in the Labor Action Plan, which included

- assigning 95 additional full-time judicial police investigators to support the investigations of criminal cases involving union members and activists;
- analyzing closed cases of union member homicides to determine patterns relating to targets, criminal methods, and any evidence of motives;
- identifying budgetary needs for training investigators and prosecutors on issues related to labor cases; and
- instructing investigators to determine whether a homicide victim was an active or retired union member, or was actively engaged in union

formation and organization, during the initial phase of the investigation.

According to the Office of the U.S. Trade Representative (USTR) and the Department of Labor (DOL), in accordance with Colombia's Labor Action Plan commitments, the Colombian government has implemented changes to a number of institutions and programs. For example, union members, in addition to union leaders, are now included in the UNP's jurisdiction. As of April 2014, the UNP protects more than 670 unionists, with about 24 percent of its budget dedicated to the protection of unionists and labor activists.

Additionally, USTR has reported that the Colombian government reformed the risk assessment process at the UNP and eliminated the backlog of hundreds of applicants to the protection program. During our fieldwork in Colombia, UNP officials described changes to the risk assessment process. For example, when an application is received, instead of a single individual investigating the case, as occurred before the process's reform, a committee now conducts interviews and fieldwork to investigate the nature of the threat and determine a risk score. The case is then forwarded to another committee, comprising representatives from organized labor, other vulnerable populations, and government agencies, that determines the risk level in each case as ordinary, extraordinary, or extreme. UNP officials reported that, based on the outcome of the risk assessment, protection measures ranging from providing a cell phone to providing an armored car and armed bodyguards are taken. State's 2013 Human Rights Report notes that between January 1 and October 31, 2013, the UNP conducted 565 risk assessments of union leaders or members. Of those, the UNP classified 203, about 36 percent, as having an extraordinary threat or extreme threat and provided the leaders or members with protection measures. According to UNP officials, prior to the Labor Action Plan–related reforms, about 10 to 15 percent of risk applicants were determined to be under extraordinary or extreme risk. Additionally, according to State, approximately one-half of the unionists enrolled in the program were provided with "hard" protection measures that included a bodyguard.

According to USTR, Colombia increased the budget of its Prosecutor General's Office, in part to investigate and prosecute cases involving union members or labor activists as victims. Further, USTR has reported that the Prosecutor General's Office has issued a mandate that assigned over 20 prosecutors exclusively to crimes against union members and labor activists. In addition, the National Police have assigned an additional 100 full-time judicial police investigators to support the prosecutors in investigating cases involving union members and labor activists. To implement the Labor Action Plan commitments to identify and effectively prosecute intellectual authors of labor homicides, the Prosecutor General's Office created a context and analysis directorate tasked with investigating the patterns and context of similar cases, including labor homicides. Officials from this unit we met with during our fieldwork in Colombia described the unit as taking an integrated approach to analyzing cases across the spectrum of human rights crimes to determine common themes and perpetrators.

Despite the actions Colombia has taken to reduce violence against union members and labor activists, Colombian union and NGO officials, as well as USTR officials, report that violence and impunity remain problems. Union members we met with during our fieldwork in Colombia reported the existence of a high impunity rate for violent crimes against unionists. According to DOL, of the 100 unionist murders that have occurred since 2011, Colombia's Prosecutor General's Office has obtained only one conviction. Union officials we met with acknowledged that the government of Colombia has taken positive steps to address violence, that the number of labor-related homicides has decreased, and that reforms have been implemented at the UNP. However, they also reported they are concerned for their safety because of their union activities. Additionally, union officials voiced the concern that risk was not being assessed at the UNP in a way that accurately captured the dangers union leaders and members face. UNP officials we met acknowledged that two union leaders who were receiving "light" protection were murdered and another union leader was murdered while he awaited the UNP's risk assessment.

U.S. Government Has Provided Assistance to Colombia to Address Violence, Including Violence against Unionists

In support of reducing violence in Colombia, including violence against unionists, U.S. agencies have funded multiple assistance projects. According to U.S. Agency for International Development (USAID) officials, from 2001 to 2010, the agency provided about $11.6 million in funding through its Human Rights fund to establish and support Colombia's UNP. The UNP, which is under the Colombian Ministry of Interior, received between 10 and 18 percent of its total annual budget from USAID funding from 2001 to 2005 (ranging from about $916,000 in 2001 to about $2.5 million in 2005). According to USAID, its assistance for the UNP has steadily decreased as budget support from the government of Colombia and the effectiveness of the

UNP have increased. For example, from 2011 to 2014, USAID provided approximately $150,000 per year in assistance to the UNP.

In support of Colombia's Labor Action Plan commitment to seek cooperation, advice, and technical assistance of the International Labour Organization (ILO), DOL is currently funding a 5-year (2011 to 2016), $7.82 million technical cooperation project implemented by the ILO. The objectives of this project include strengthening the institutional capacity of the Colombian government to enhance protection measures for trade union leaders, members, activists, and organizers and combating impunity for perpetrators of violence against them. Under this project, the ILO is training Colombian prosecutors, investigators, and judges on labor rights and investigating crimes against union leaders and labor activists. In addition, Colombia's Prosecutor General's Office officials reported that the office has received assistance from the U.S. Department of Justice on broad criminal justice reforms, including transitioning from an inquisitorial to an accusatory legal system. USTR reports that State has funded, and the Department of Justice has implemented, assistance to train investigators and prosecutors throughout Colombia in best practices for crime scene investigation, including forensic evidence handling, investigating threats, and prosecutorial management of cases for trial. The Department of Justice's and State's programs are aimed at broader criminal justice reform; however, Colombia's Prosecutor General's Office reported to us that the reforms apply to investigating and prosecuting violence against unionists.

Guatemala

Instances of Violence and Threats of Violence against Trade Unionists Have Been Reported in Guatemala

U.S. and Guatemalan government officials and ILO and union representatives reported that violence against unionists exists in Guatemala; however, the extent of the problem is unclear because disaggregated statistics on violence against unionists are not collected. Nevertheless, a union collected information on 63 cases in which union leaders or members were killed from 2007 through 2013. The unions alleged that the motive for these murders was related to the victims' union activities and that the government of Guatemala has not done enough to investigate and resolve the cases. In addition, ILO officials stated that they have detailed extremely serious and systematic violations of the right to freedom of association in Guatemala, including murder.

A 2012 ILO complaint against the Guatemalan government cited 63 murders of trade unionists and called for the establishment of an ILO commission of inquiry.[4] Guatemalan officials confirmed that violence against trade unionists exists but reported that many of the cases cited in the ILO complaint were the result of general, extensive violence and crime in the country rather than violence directed against trade unionists. According to Ministry of the Interior officials, the ministry's initial investigation of the 63 murder cases was unable to identify any link between the perpetrators' motives and the victims' union activity. Furthermore, as part of a cooperative agreement with the Guatemalan Attorney General's Office, the International Commission against Impunity in Guatemala (CICIG) began a review of the 58 cases cited in the ILO complaint to ensure the adequacy of the investigations.[5] According to DOL, as of June 2014, CICIG had completed its review of 56 cases and concluded that 6 of the cases indicated a possible link to union activity.

In addition, unions reported other violent acts, such as threats, bribes, and intimidation against union members. According to union representatives we interviewed, threats of violence begin with harassing phone calls to a union leader or member. The union representative stated that if the phone calls do not get the desired results, the harassment is escalated to include physical intimidation and threats of kidnapping. If the physical intimidation fails, then kidnapping or murder occurs.

Guatemala Has Taken Steps to Prevent and Investigate Violence against Unionists in Response to ILO Review

To address the complaint filed by the unions, the ILO initiated the process to establish commissions of inquiry. To avoid the establishment of the commission, the government of Guatemala signed a memorandum of understanding in March of 2013, committing to take specific steps to address the issues in the complaint and establishing a plan called the Road Map that outlined the actions needed. In response, the ILO decided to postpone the establishment of the Commission of Inquiry and has been working with Guatemala to implement the Road Map.

According to information that the government of Guatemala provided to the ILO, as of March of 2014, steps that the government had taken to address violence against unionists included

- a cooperative agreement signed with the International CICIG to support the Public Prosecutor's Office in analyzing cases of violence against trade unionists;
- the transfer of 20 trained investigators to the Attorney General's Office and the creation of the new post of assistant prosecutor in the special unit investigating crimes against trade unionists;
- improvement in the time periods for trial and convictions, including those for some of the 58 murders reported to the ILO; and
- submission by the Ministry of the Interior, in the context of analyzing assaults on trade unionists, of a draft protocol for implementing immediate and preventive security measures for trade union leaders, unionized workers, and workers from trade unions in the process of being established.

Following are descriptions of some of the Guatemalan government's ongoing efforts to address violence against trade unionists.

Cooperative Agreement with CICIG

According to a March 2014 ILO report, the Guatemalan Attorney General's Office signed a cooperative agreement with CICIG on September 24, 2013.[6] As part of the agreement, the Attorney General's Office established a coordination mechanism with CICIG for the analysis of specific cases of violence against trade union members. CICIG agreed to support the Attorney General's Office in the analysis of specific cases of violence against union members, providing recommendations to strengthen the investigation of those cases. Under the new coordination mechanism, the 58 murder cases cited in the ILO complaint were transferred to CICIG to continue the investigation process. In addition, the Attorney General agreed to cooperate with CICIG in the analysis of crime trends based on landmark cases of attacks and violence against union members known to the different units and offices of the Public Prosecutor's Office.

Additional Trained Investigators

The Ministry of the Interior and the Attorney General's Office established interinstitutional links for cooperation to strengthen the investigations and criminal prosecution. Through this mechanism, the Ministry of the Interior transferred 20 trained investigators to the Attorney General's Office, with the effort to provide additional support to investigate cases of violence against unionists.

Timely Trials and Convictions

The government of Guatemala has worked to improve the length of time it takes to bring perpetrators of crimes to trial and issue convictions. In regard to the 58 murder cases cited in the ILO complaint, the Attorney General's Office provided an update of the status of the 28 cases that have been brought to court and reported that extinction of criminal liability has been applied in 4 cases, arrest warrants have been issued in 13 cases, rulings have been handed down in 6 cases, and 5 cases are pending trial.[7]

Strengthening Analysis of Attacks against Human Rights Defenders

The Attorney General's Office restructured and strengthened the unit that analyzes attacks against human rights defenders, a category that includes unionists. As part of this process, representatives of unionized workers will meet regularly to study trends in attacks against human rights defenders and draw up recommendations for investigations by the Attorney General Office to assist both criminal investigations and the conviction of the perpetrators. An adequately staffed office will be created to carry out the relevant investigations.

The government of Guatemala reported several other steps it intends to initiate or has initiated to address the issues in the ILO complaint. For example, according to the ILO's March 2014 report, the Ministry of Labor and Social Welfare proposed amendments to the Labor Code and other relevant laws, incorporating the amendments proposed by the ILO supervisory bodies.[8] The ILO's report stated that legislative reforms have also been proposed by the Ministry of Labor to enable the general labor inspectorate to fulfill its mandate to ensure the effective application of labor legislation. On the basis of the progress demonstrated in addressing points in the Road Map reported by the government of Guatemala, the ILO decided in March 2014 to again postpone the implementation of the Commission of Inquiry and reevaluate progress in November of 2014.

U.S. Government Has Provided Assistance to Guatemala for Law Enforcement Reform and to Address Violence, Including Violence against Unionists

The United States has provided some funding through State's Bureau of International Narcotics and Law Enforcement (INL) to assist Guatemalan authorities to provide better protection to unionists. INL provided Guatemala $2 million dollars in assistance for fiscal years 2012 through 2016 to implement reform and capacity-building projects. The goal of the INL funding is to increase the investigative capabilities of law enforcement officers within the Ministry of the Interior. Part of the funding focuses on defenders of human rights, including addressing violence against trade unions. Assistance provided by INL has ranged from the provision of equipment to technical training and exchanges. For example, INL provided the Ministry of the Interior's recently established security division, División de Protección de Personas y Seguridad (DPPS), with filing cabinets to organize files on union leaders for which it was providing protection. INL officials stated that DPPS lacked a tracking system and had rooms stacked with disorganized files and, as a result, could not accurately track the number of people receiving protection. According to INL officials, as of December 2013, DPPS was providing protection for about 1,000 union leaders and members. INL officials also stated that they had discussed the possibility of creating a risk analysis unit in DPPS, similar to Colombia's UNP.

APPENDIX III: U.S. MONITORING OF IMPLEMENTATION OF OTHER LABOR INITIATIVES

In addition to being responsible for monitoring partner countries' implementation of free trade agreement (FTA) labor provisions, U.S. agencies are responsible for monitoring the implementation of labor initiatives such as the White Paper[1] and the Labor Action Plan,[2] which were developed in the context of, respectively, the Dominican Republic-Central America-United States Free Trade Agreement (CAFTA-DR) and the United States-Colombia Trade Promotion Agreement (Colombia FTA).[3] U.S. agencies are also responsible for monitoring Guatemala's Labor Enforcement Plan, developed in response to a CAFTA-DR labor submission to the Department of Labor (DOL).[4]

CAFTA-DR White Paper

To discharge its responsibility for monitoring implementation of the CAFTA-DR White Paper projects, in 2007 DOL provided a $10 million grant to the International Labour Organization's (ILO) Verification Project.[5] The Verification Project prepared reports every 6 months from 2005 through 2010 regarding the implementation of the White Paper projects. The Verification Project and most White Paper projects concluded in 2012.

The ILO Verification Project tracked spending and implementation of every White Paper project, requiring grant recipients to submit periodic reports to ILO for the biannual report. ILO staff provided the reports to DOL, which used the reports to ensure transparency and progress of the U.S.-funded projects. Entities implementing White Paper projects included, among others, the U.S. Agency for International Development (USAID), partner countries' ministries of labor and labor courts, and nongovernmental organizations. According to ILO staff, although the Verification Project did not measure the impact of the projects on labor conditions, the reports reflected improvements of government institutions and other entities and demonstrated the benefit of addressing some issues faced by workers. ILO officials noted that, besides providing accountability for the expenditure of funds and tracking the progress of projects, the Verification Project led to improvements in data gathering and reporting capabilities of the ministries of labor.

Colombia Labor Action Plan

The Office of the U.S. Trade Representative (USTR), in cooperation with DOL and the Department of State (State), is responsible for monitoring the implementation of the Colombia Labor Action Plan, most of which Colombia was required to implement by 2012. The plan listed steps to improve labor conditions, mutually agreed on by the U.S. and Colombian governments, that the Colombian government agreed to take before the President of the United States would put the FTA forward for congressional consideration. The conditions that the Labor Action Plan addressed included violence against Colombian labor union members, inadequate efforts to bring to justice perpetrators of crimes against labor union members, and insufficient protection of workers' rights in Colombia. According to USTR staff, the plan continues to serve as a framework for cooperation with Colombia. The plan includes regular meetings between officials from both countries to monitor and implement the plan through 2013, and both governments announced an extension of these meetings through at least 2014.

On April 2012, USTR announced that the Colombian government had taken important steps to fulfill the Labor Action Plan and that the FTA would go into effect. USTR officials did not provide records or documentation of these steps, stating that they did not request such records because the website for the Presidency of Colombia supplied documentation of all actions taken. On reviewing some of the documentation on the website, we found that the documents were not structured so as to readily provide information about steps that the Colombian government had taken to meet its Labor Action Plan commitments. In written responses to our questions, Colombia's Ministry of Labor indicated that the government had met all Labor Action Plan commitments, and the ministry provided examples of the government's actions to meet these commitments.

USTR officials reported that USTR, DOL, and State had engaged extensively with the Colombian Ministry of Labor and other government institutions in Colombia to discuss and confirm Colombia's progress in implementing each element of the Labor Action Plan. According to USTR, as of August 2014, USTR and DOL staff had made seven visits to Colombia since the FTA entered into force to address these issues. USTR fact sheets and a USTR and DOL report from April 2014 provided information about Colombia's accomplishments under the Labor Action Plan—for example, the report detailed the number of labor inspectors hired, the number of special prosecutors and investigators hired, and the number of convictions in cases of violence against labor leaders—as well as remaining challenges. In addition, according to DOL, a DOL staff member, detailed to the U.S. embassy in Bogota from 2011 to 2012 to oversee implementation of the Action Plan, met during that period with Colombian government officials, nongovernmental organizations, union representatives, and other stakeholders to discuss the Labor Action Plan's implementation, among other topics.

Guatemala Enforcement Plan

USTR, in cooperation with DOL and State, is responsible for monitoring implementation of the Guatemala Enforcement Plan, agreed to by the U.S. and Guatemalan governments in April 2013, to address concerns identified in a labor submission filed under CAFTA-DR. USTR provided us with internal documents that it had used to track Guatemala's progress in taking the steps required by the plan. For example, USTR provided a matrix tracking the status of legal instruments required under the Enforcement Plan; USTR also provided quarterly progress reports submitted by the Guatemalan Ministry of Labor, identifying steps that the ministry had taken to address commitments in the Enforcement Plan. USTR officials said that since 2009, USTR and DOL had directly engaged with Guatemala on the labor case through 17 trips, including 7 trips that involved staff at the Assistant Secretary level or higher. In addition, officials at the Guatemalan Ministry of Labor told us that they had interacted extensively with DOL and USTR, including through multiple video-teleconferences, meetings in person, and correspondence, to update them on progress in implementing the Enforcement Plan.

In April 2014, USTR told us that although it recognized steps that Guatemala had taken under the Enforcement Plan, it had not seen sufficient progress to close the case. USTR officials stated that if the Guatemalan government did not take the steps delineated in the plan by the specified dates, USTR might decide to pursue arbitration. In September 2014, USTR announced that the U.S. government was pursuing dispute settlement proceedings against Guatemala because it had not met the terms of the Enforcement Plan.

APPENDIX IV: STATUS OF LABOR SUBMISSIONS

The following provides details about the status of the five labor submissions that the Department of Labor (DOL) has accepted since 2008.[1]

Bahrain

In June 2011, DOL accepted a labor submission regarding Bahrain, 50 days after receipt. The submission remains open, with consultations ongoing. The submission, received from the American Federation of Labor and Congress of Industrial Organizations (AFL-CIO) with a statement from the General Federation of Bahrain Trade Unions, alleged that Bahrain had violated free trade agreement (FTA) labor provisions regarding the right of association, particularly nondiscrimination against trade unionists. In December 2012, DOL issued a public report that found that the government of Bahrain's actions appeared inconsistent with its commitments under the labor chapter. Specifically, the report found that trade unionists and leaders were targeted for dismissal, and in some cases prosecuted, in part for their role in organizing and participating in a general strike and that the dismissals reflected discrimination based in part on political opinion and activities. The report also found sectarian discrimination against Shia workers. The Department of Labor's (DOL) report outlined nine recommendations focused on legal and administrative changes to Bahraini labor law for the U.S. government to pursue during consultations with Bahrain and also recommended that the parties develop a plan of action.

On May 6, 2013, more than 4 months after DOL issued its report, the U.S. government formally requested cooperative labor consultations with the government of Bahrain in a joint letter from the Acting Secretary of Labor and the Acting U.S. Trade Representative. Consultations began when an interagency delegation met with the government of Bahrain in Manama, Bahrain, on July 15 and 16, 2013. However, according to DOL, the first round of consultations did not resolve all issues DOL had identified, and consultations were ongoing as of September 2014. The Office of the U.S. Trade Representative (USTR) attempted to schedule second-round consultations but agreed to a request from Bahrain to delay them. The United States and Bahrain held a second round of consultations on June 22 and 23, 2014, according to DOL. During the consultations, the two parties used the recommendations in the DOL report as a basis for jointly developing an action plan, which includes concrete steps for the government of Bahrain to address the concerns that the report raises. USTR officials noted that the allegations raised in the submission are subject to resolution through the consultation procedures but are not subject to dispute settlement.[2]

Figure 5 shows the timeline and status of the Bahrain labor submission.

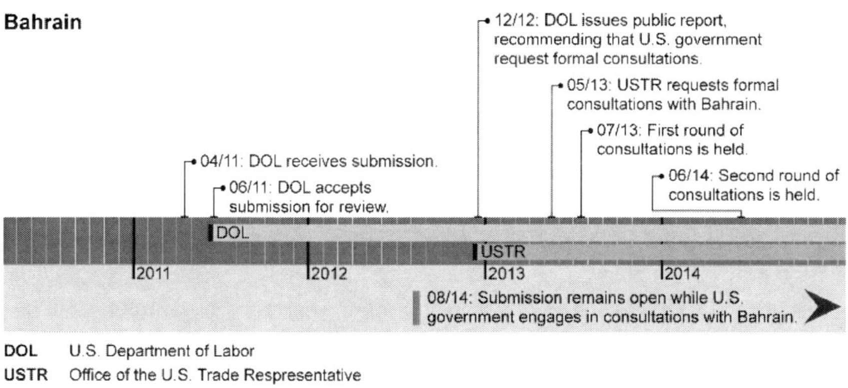

Source: GAO analysis of Department of Labor information. l GAO-15-160.
Legend: DOL = U.S. Department of Labor.

Figure 5. Timeline and Status of Labor Submission Regarding Bahrain.

Dominican Republic

In February 2012, DOL accepted a labor submission regarding the Dominican Republic, 62 days after receipt. The submission remains open and unresolved while DOL monitors the Dominican Republic's progress in addressing concerns that the submission raises. The submission, submitted by a private individual, alleged the failure of the Dominican Republic's government to enforce its labor laws in the sugar sector as required under the Dominican Republic-Central America-United States Free Trade Agreement (CAFTA-DR). The submission alleged nine violations, ranging from human trafficking and forced labor to retaliatory firing of workers for affiliation with, or attempts to organize, labor groups or unions. In September 2013, DOL issued a public report that found evidence of apparent and potential violations of the Dominican Republic's labor laws pertaining to the sugar sector. DOL's report also identified significant concerns about procedural and methodological shortcomings in the inspection process that undermine the government's capacity to effectively identify labor violations. In addition, the report cited concerns regarding freedom of association, the right to organize, and collective bargaining. DOL's report offered 11 recommendations to the government of the Dominican Republic to address the report's findings and improve enforcement of Dominican labor laws in the sugar sector and stated that DOL would reassess the situation in 6 and 12 months after the report's publication. The recommendations range from administrative changes to help the government of the Dominican Republic improve its enforcement of Dominican labor laws to outreach suggestions for better informing sugar sector workers about their labor rights.

In April 2014, DOL issued its 6-month assessment, noting that the Dominican Republic's Ministry of Labor had committed to measures that, if instituted, would begin to address some of the recommendations in DOL's public report. DOL's assessment also noted that the government of the Dominican Republic had not yet indicated plans or taken actions to address most of the public report's recommendations.

Figure 6 shows the timeline and status of the Dominican Republic labor submission.

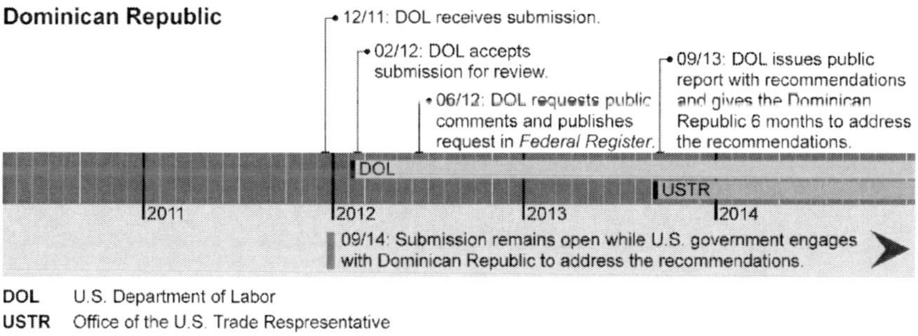

Source: GAO analysis of Department of Labor information. | GAO-15-160.
Legend: DOL = U.S. Department of Labor.

Figure 6. Timeline and Status of Labor Submission Regarding the Dominican Republic.

Guatemala

In June 2008, DOL accepted a submission regarding Guatemala, 50 days after receipt. The submission remains open and unresolved and is currently in arbitration. The submission, from the AFL-CIO and six Guatemalan worker organizations, alleged that Guatemala had violated its obligation under CAFTA-DR to effectively enforce its labor laws regarding freedom of association, the rights to organize and bargain collectively, and acceptable conditions of work. In January 2009, DOL issued a public report that found significant weaknesses in Guatemala's labor law enforcement. The report outlined 10 recommendations for the government of Guatemala, including administrative and technical changes, to address the issues raised in the submission. The report also recommended that DOL reassess Guatemala's progress in implementing the recommendations within 6 months after the publication of DOL's report to determine whether further action is warranted.

USTR and DOL engaged with the Guatemalan government in an effort to address DOL's recommendations for systemic improvements in the enforcement of labor laws in Guatemala. In July 2010, after Guatemala's actions proved insufficient to address the concerns raised in the report, USTR and DOL jointly requested cooperative labor consultations with Guatemala under the CAFTA-DR Labor Chapter.

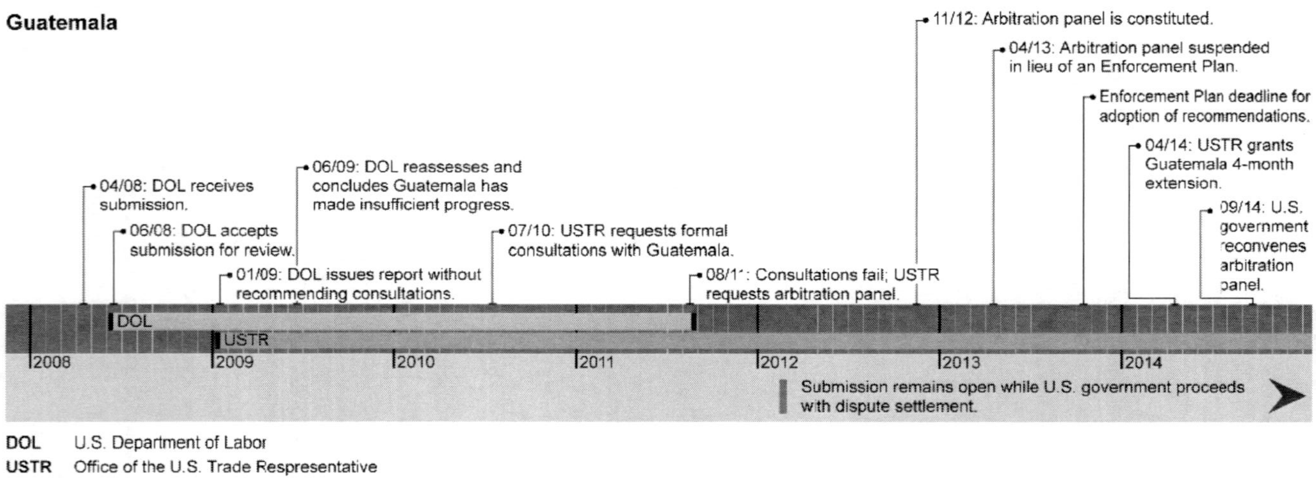

Source: GAO analysis of Department of Labor information. | GAO-15-160.

Legend: DOL = U.S. Department of Labor; CAFTA-DR = United States-Dominican Republic-Central America Free Trade Agreement.

Figure 7. Timeline and Status of Labor Submission Regarding Guatemala.

The consultations failed to resolve the matter, and on May 16, 2011, USTR requested a meeting of the CAFTA-DR's free trade commission pursuant to the agreement's Dispute Settlement Chapter. The commission met in June 2011 but did not resolve the dispute, and in August 2011, the United States requested the establishment of an arbitral panel. After the panel was constituted in November 2012, the parties agreed to suspend it to allow for additional negotiation. In April 2013, the parties reached agreement on a comprehensive 18-point Enforcement Plan with concrete benchmarks and timelines for implementation. The plan extended the arbitration panel's suspension for 6 months, with the possibility of an additional 6- month extension based on Guatemala's progress in implementing the plan. In October 2013, 6 months after the signing of the Enforcement Plan, USTR, in consultation with DOL, determined that Guatemala had taken sufficient steps to enact the legal instruments called for under the plan. USTR and DOL granted the 6-month extension, noting that significant work remained to ensure the full implementation of the Enforcement Plan.

In April 2014, USTR, in consultation with DOL, granted Guatemala a 4-month extension to continue its implementation of the Enforcement Plan but retains the right to reactivate the arbitration panel at any point during this period. In September 2014, the United States reactivated the panel after determining that Guatemala had not met the terms of the Enforcement Plan and that concerns over the enforcement of Guatemala's labor laws had not been resolved.

Figure 7 shows the timeline and status of the Guatemala labor submission.

Honduras

In May 2012, DOL accepted a submission regarding Honduras, 49 days after receipt. The submission remains open and unresolved, pending publication of DOL's report. The submission, from the AFL-CIO and 26 Honduran organizations, alleged that the government of Honduras had violated its obligation under CAFTA-DR to enforce its labor laws relating to freedom of association; the right to organize; child labor; the right to bargain collectively; and the right to acceptable conditions of work in the Honduran apparel and auto manufacturing, agriculture, and port sectors. According to DOL officials, DOL has received over 1,200 documents in Spanish and visited Honduras four times to meet with stakeholders, reflecting the breadth of the allegations and detailed information reviewed and analyzed. As of May 2014,

DOL was continuing to review documentation of the allegations and, according to DOL officials, is preparing its report.

Figure 8 shows the timeline and status of the Honduras labor submission.

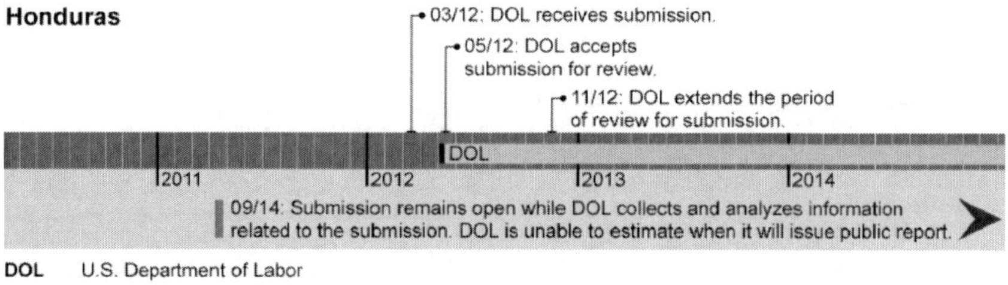

Source: GAO analysis of Department of Labor information. | GAO-15-160.
Legend: DOL = U.S. Department of Labor.

Figure 8. Timeline and Status of Labor Submission Regarding Honduras.

Peru

In July 2011, DOL accepted a submission regarding Peru, 202 days after receipt, which DOL closed as resolved in August 2012. The submission, from the Peruvian National Union of Tax Administration Workers (SINAUT), alleged that Peru's National Superintendency of Tax Administration (SUNAT), an executive branch agency of the Peruvian government that oversees both customs and tax administration, had failed to comply with Peru's labor laws as they relate to collective bargaining, in violation of the United States-Peru Trade Promotion Agreement. In August 2012, DOL issued a public report finding that although the Ministry of Labor and Promotion of Employment appeared to have fulfilled its duties during the collective bargaining processes at issue, SUNAT had failed to comply with certain elements of the Peruvian Collective Bargaining Law, including deadlines for launching negotiations. Further, with regard to all other issues raised in the submission, DOL determined that important legal ambiguity during the period at issue prevented a finding that SUNAT had failed to comply with the law or that the government of Peru had failed to comply with, or enforce, its own labor laws during that time. DOL's report did not recommend formal consultations between the U.S. government and the Peruvian government. According to DOL, because the government of Peru had taken important steps to address some of the issues raised in the submission, including issuing legal instruments to help clarify legal ambiguity and facilitate collective bargaining,

DOL did not believe that formal consultations were needed to continue positive engagement and progress on these matters. As a result, DOL closed the submission as resolved in August 2012.

In September 2011, according to DOL, while it was reviewing the submission, the government of Peru issued two executive orders that clarified the parties' collective bargaining duties in this and similar cases. DOL's report on the submission explained that on March 29, 2012, after applying the recent executive orders, an arbitral panel reached a decision favorable to SINAUT that contained both economic and noneconomic awards for the union. Moreover, DOL reported that the government of Peru appealed the ruling, contending that the ruling reflects a misapplication and misinterpretation of the Public Sector Budget Law. According to the DOL report, on appeal, the Peruvian labor courts overturned the economic elements of the arbitral award, based on a ruling that those elements conflicted with Peru's Public Sector Budget Law, but sustained the noneconomic elements of the award.

Figure 9 shoes the timeline and status of the Peru labor submission.

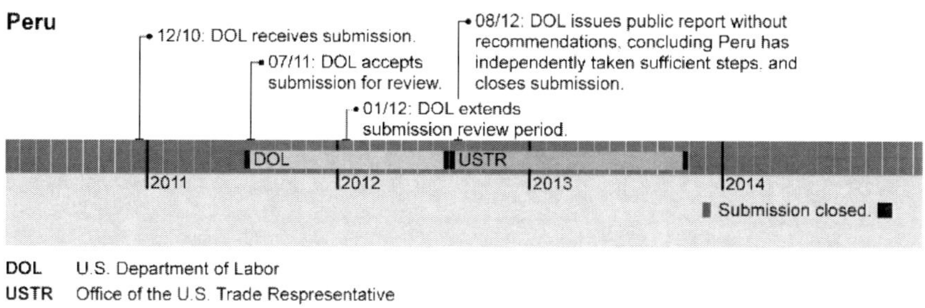

Source: GAO analysis of Department of Labor information. I GAO-15-160.

Legend: DOL = U.S. Department of Labor; USTR = Office of the U.S. Trade Representative.

Figure 9. Timeline and Status of Labor Submission Regarding Peru.

End Notes

[1] For example, FTAs that have entered into force since February 2009 contain a provision stating that "[e]ach Party shall adopt and maintain in its statutes and regulations, and practices thereunder, the following rights, as stated in the ILO [International Labour Organization] Declaration on Fundamental Principles and Rights at Work and Its Follow-up (1998)." For example, see United States-Colombia FTA (entered into Force May 2012), art. 17.2. According to the Department of Labor (DOL), freedom of association is the right of workers and employers to organize to defend their interests, including for the purpose of

negotiating salaries, benefits, and other conditions of work, and is a fundamental right that underpins democratic representation and governance; collective bargaining is an essential element of freedom of association that helps to ensure that workers and employers have an equal voice in negotiations and provides workers the opportunity to seek to improve their living and working conditions.

[2] As of July 2014, the United States had entered into FTAs with Australia, Bahrain, Canada, Chile, Colombia, Costa Rica, the Dominican Republic, El Salvador, Guatemala, Honduras, Israel, Jordan, South Korea, Mexico, Morocco, Nicaragua, Oman, Panama, Peru, and Singapore. The Dominican Republic-Central America-United States Free Trade Agreement (CAFTA-DR) covers six of these countries (Costa Rica, Dominican Republic, El Salvador, Guatemala, Honduras, and Nicaragua).

[3] Trade Promotion Authority, previously known as "fast track" negotiating authority, established conditions and procedures under which the President could submit legislation to approve and implement trade agreements, such as FTAs, that Congress could approve or disapprove but could not amend or filibuster. See Bipartisan Trade Promotion Authority Act of 2002, Pub. L. No. 107-210, Div. B, § 2103, 116 Stat. 933, 1004–08.

[4] GAO, *International Trade: Four Free Trade Agreements GAO Reviewed Have Resulted in Commercial Benefits, but Challenges on Labor and Environment Remain*, GAO-09-439 (Washington, D.C.: July 10, 2009). Our 2009 report reviewed implementation of the U.S. FTAs with, respectively, Chile, Jordan, Morocco, and Singapore.

[5] Additional information about U.S. agencies' monitoring and reporting on compliance with, and progress under, FTA labor provisions is presented later in this report.

[6] According to USTR, FTA provisions provide for the FTA's entry into force through an exchange of formal diplomatic notes among the parties. USTR also notes that, in the United States, the President must first determine that the trading partner has come into compliance with obligations that will take effect when the agreement enters into force. When an FTA enters into force, it generally means that the agreement becomes legally binding on the parties to the agreement.

[7] Congressional leaders and the Bush administration jointly agreed to the May 10th Agreement, resulting in a new trade policy template that calls for, among other things, (1) enforceable reciprocal obligation for the countries to adopt and maintain in their laws and practice the five basic internationally recognized labor principles, as stated in the International Labour Organization (ILO) Declaration on Fundamental Principles and Rights at Work and (2) labor obligations subject to the same dispute settlement procedures and remedies as commercial obligations.

[8] The views expressed by these officials and organizations cannot be generalized to all officials or organizations knowledgeable about labor provisions in the selected FTAs.

[9] All of the selected FTAs contain mechanisms to address matters arising under the respective labor chapters. CAFTA-DR and the Colombia, Oman, and Peru FTAs each include labor provisions that state that each party shall designate an office within its labor ministry that shall serve as a contact point with the other party and with the public. Furthermore, the FTAs state that each party's contact point shall provide for the submission, receipt, and consideration of communications on matters related to the respective labor chapter and shall make such communications available to the other party and, as appropriate, to the public. While either party can request consultations regarding any matter addressed in the labor chapter, FTA dispute settlement procedures may be invoked only under specified circumstances, which vary by FTA.

[10] FTAs with Colombia, Panama, Peru, and South Korea contain language reflecting the labor provisions of the May 10th Agreement.

[11] United States-Singapore Free Trade Agreement (entered into force in January 2004), art. 17.2; United States-Chile Free Trade Agreement (entered into force in January 2004), art. 18.2; United States-Australia Free Trade Agreement (entered into in force January 2005), art. 18.2; United States-Morocco Free Trade Agreement (entered into force in January 2006), art. 16.2; CAFTA-DR (entered into force between 2006 and 2009 for the various countries), art. 16.2; United States-Bahrain Free Trade Agreement (Bahrain FTA) (entered into force in January 2006), art. 15.2; and Oman FTA (entered into force in January 2009), art. 16.2.

[12] CAFTA-DR, art. 16.6.7; Oman FTA art. 16.6.5.

[13] CAFTA-DR, art. 16.1.1 and 16.6.7; Oman FTA, art. 16.1.1 and 16.6.5.

[14] United States-Peru FTA (entered into force in February 2009), art. 17.2, 17.3; United States-Colombia FTA (entered into force in May 2012), art. 17.2, 17.3; United States-Korea Free Trade Agreement (entered into force in March 2012), art. 19.2, 19.3; and United States-Panama Free Trade Agreement (entered into force in October 2012), art. 16.2, 16.3.

[15] International Labour Organization, *Declaration on Fundamental Principles and Rights at Work and Its Follow-Up* (1998), http://www.ilo.org/declaration/thedeclaration /textdeclaration /lang--en/index.htm, accessed August 18, 2014. The principles and rights stated by the ILO are (1) freedom of association and the effective recognition of the right to collective bargaining, (2) the elimination of all forms of forced or compulsory labor, (3) the effective abolition of child labor, and (4) the elimination of discrimination in respect of employment and occupation.

[16] United States-Peru FTA, art. 17.7; Colombia FTA, art. 17.7; United States-Korea Free Trade Agreement, art. 19.7; and United States-Panama Free Trade Agreement, art. 16.7.

[17] Working Group of the Vice Ministers Responsible for Trade and Labor in the Countries of Central America and the Dominican Republic, *The Labor Dimension in Central America and the Dominican Republic: Building on Progress: Strengthening Compliance and Enhancing Capacity* (April 2005), accessed June 7, 2013, http://www.ilo.org/sanjose /lang—es/index.htm.

[18] *Colombian Action Plan Related to Labor Rights* (April 7, 2011), accessed May 29, 2013, http://www.ustr.gov/webfm_send/2787.

[19] These labor initiatives were created outside an FTA framework.

[20] Dominican Republic-Central America-United States Free Trade Agreement Implementation Act, Pub. L. No. 109-53, 119 Stat. 262 (Aug. 2, 2005).

[21] Under the White Paper, the labor ministers of the six CAFTA-DR countries agreed to address the following priority areas: (1) labor law and implementation, (2) budget and personnel needs of the labor ministries, (3) strengthening the judicial system for labor law, (4) protections against discrimination in the workplace, (5) worst forms of child labor, and (6) promoting a culture of compliance.

[22] The nine areas that Colombia agreed to address under the Labor Action Plan were (1) creation of a specialized Ministry of Labor; (2) criminal code reform; (3) prohibiting the misuse of cooperatives; (4) preventing the use of temporary service agencies to circumvent labor rights; (5) criminalizing the use of collective pacts to undermine the right to organize and bargain collectively; (6) collecting and disseminating information on the definition of essential services; (7) seeking the ILO's assistance in implementing the Labor Action Plan and working with the ILO to strengthen its presence, capacity, and role in Colombia; (8) reforming protection programs; and (9) criminal justice reforms.

[23] 19 U.S.C. § 2171. Generally, the trade agreements program includes all activities consisting of, or related to, the negotiation or administration of international agreements that primarily concern trade and that are concluded pursuant to the authority vested in the President by the Constitution, 19 U.S.C. § 1351, the Trade Expansion Act of 1962, and the Trade Act of 1974 as amended.

[24] In addition, DOL is responsible for convening the FTA labor affairs councils among partner government's labor ministries, which oversee the FTA labor chapters, and for administering the U.S. Labor Advisory Committee for Trade Negotiations and Trade Policy. The committee consists of representatives of labor organizations and is tasked with providing information and advice with respect to negotiation and implementation of U.S. trade agreements. DOL also administers the National Advisory Committee for Labor Provisions of U.S. Free Trade Agreements, which consists of 12 representatives (4 from the business community, 4 from the labor community, and 4 from the public sector).

[25] Department of Labor, *Progress in Implementing Chapter 16 (Labor) and Capacity-Building under the Dominican Republic-Central America-United States Free Trade Agreement* (Washington D.C.: May 11, 2012). According to DOL, this report relies on information collected by the ILO as part of its project to verify the results of actions taken to address the White Paper recommendations.

[26] Stakeholders reported challenges related to the issuance of fines, as discussed later in this report

[27] *Mutually Agreed Enforcement Action Plan between the Government of the United States and the Government of Guatemala* (2013), accessed August 1, 2013, http://www.dol.gov/ilab/programs/otla/guatemalasub.htm.

[28] The commitments outlined in the Enforcement Plan are (1) reaching an interagency information exchange agreement, (2) providing police assistance for Ministry of Labor inspectors, (3) allocating resources for Ministry of Labor enforcement of labor laws, (4) allowing for the ministry to issue fine recommendations and expedited judicial review, (5) standardizing time frames for Ministry of Labor inspections, (6) ensuring labor law compliance for certain enterprises, (7) ensuring labor law compliance for enterprises receiving export benefits, (8) ensuring labor law compliance upon enterprise closure, (9) employer substitution, (10) developing a system for tracking compliance with court orders, (11) verifying employer compliance with court orders, (12) monitoring judicial enforcement of court orders, (13) applying certain labor code articles, (14) ensuring transparency and tripartite coordination on Enforcement Plan implementation, (15) publishing labor law enforcement statistics and data.

[29] According to DOL, associated work cooperatives are self-governed, autonomous enterprises, under which associated workers are considered cooperative owners, rather than workers, and are excluded from many Labor Code protections.

[30] According to DOL's 2011 *Labor Rights Report on Colombia,* until late 2010, penalties for the misuse of cooperatives to avoid direct employment relationships were not enforced against third-party employers. According to DOL, as a result, cooperatives became a vehicle widely used by employers to end direct employment relationships with their workforces while retaining the same workers through cooperatives and continuing to act as their de facto employers.

[31] This amount includes both FTA and non-FTA labor-related assistance provided to FTA partner countries. This amount does not include labor-related technical assistance to Oman that DOL provided for a joint project in Oman and Bahrain. DOL's records show that it obligated $758,000 for the project in 2006 but do not show how the funds were divided

between the two countries, because, according to DOL, standard financial reports for federal grants to more than one country do not allow the grantor to report amounts received by each country. In addition, this amount excludes any assistance provided under the United States-Israel Free Trade Agreement (Israel FTA), which does not contain a specific article on labor provisions, and the North American Free Trade Agreement (NAFTA), which addresses labor-related issues under a related agreement, the North American Agreement on Labor Cooperation.

[32] This amount excludes the Israel FTA and NAFTA.

[33] Beginning in 2005, Congress appropriated funds for labor-capacity-building activities relating to the free trade agreements with the countries of Central America and the Dominican Republic. For example, see Consolidated Appropriations Act, 2005, Pub. L. No.108-447, §570, 118 Stat. 2809, 3026 (2004).

[34] According to USTR, as of September 2014, this bill had not been passed by the Guatemalan congress.

[35] For more information about the status of implementation of the Guatemala Enforcement Plan, see app. III.

[36] According to U.S and Guatemalan officials, as well as union representatives and the ILO, violence against unionists has occurred in Guatemala. The government of Guatemala reported that it had taken steps to address the violence. However, stakeholders were unsure of the extent of the problem because of a lack of statistics collected by the government. For more information about violence against unionists in Guatemala, see app. II.

[37] According to DOL, Colombia's Minister of Labor heads SENA's board of directors.

[38] According to DOL, a simplified stock company is a corporate model that holds shareholders liable only up to the amount of their investment. DOL further stated that these companies are easy to create and dissolve and are a legitimate business model in Colombia. In cases where a simplified stock company is used for contracting—either legal or illegal—an employer hires the company to carry out a task and the company provides the labor through its own employees.

[39] In addition, although murders of unionists have generally been decreasing over the past 10 years, and despite actions by the Colombian government to reduce homicides of union members and labor activists, stakeholders we interviewed reported that violence against unionists continues. For a more detailed description of reported violence against union members and activists in Colombia, see app. II.

[40] According to State, Peru's nontraditional export sectors include fishing, wood and paper, nonmetallic minerals, jewelry, textiles and apparel, and the agriculture industry.

[41] According to DOL officials, DOL also received a sixth submission, filed under the Costa Rica FTA in July 2010, which the filing party withdrew before DOL decided whether to accept it. DOL has also accepted other labor submissions under the North American Agreement on Labor Cooperation (one of three accords supplementary to NAFTA), which we did not examine.

[42] 71 Fed. Reg. 76691 (Dec. 21, 2006).

[43] DOL has also accepted other labor submissions under the North American Agreement on Labor Cooperation (one of three accords supplementary to NAFTA), which we did not examine.

[44] DOL may extend the timeframe if it determines that the circumstances require such an extension. 71 Fed. Reg. 76691.

[45] GAO, *Auditing and Financial Management: Standards for Internal Control in the Federal Government*, AIMD-00-21.3.1 (Washington, D.C.: Nov. 1, 1999).

[46] The American Center for International Labor Solidarity, better known as the Solidarity Center, is a nonprofit organization affiliated with the AFL-CIO labor federation whose mission is to help build a global labor movement by strengthening the economic and political power of workers around the world through effective, independent, and democratic unions.

[47] AIMD-00-21.3.1.

[48] U.S. Department of Labor, *Submissions under the Labor Provisions of Free Trade Agreements*, accessed Aug. 5, 2014, http://www.dol.gov/ilab/trade/agreements/ftasubs.htm. See also, 71 Fed. Reg. 76691.

[49] The labor chapters of some FTAs call for the establishment of a bilateral labor affairs council to oversee, and review progress in, implementation of the labor chapter's provisions.

[50] In commenting on a draft of this report, DOL noted that during its submission review, the partner government has the opportunity to provide input and DOL visits the partner country and reviews any information that the partner government provides. DOL also noted that the submission review process is a fact-finding exercise intended to evaluate the merits of allegations raised in a submission and that acceptance of a submission for review does not imply that the allegations are correct. In addition, DOL stated that its decision to review a public submission does not indicate any determination as to the validity or accuracy of the allegations contained in the submission; instead, the submission's merit is addressed in the public report that follows DOL's review and analysis. According to DOL, after its submission review report is issued, USTR and DOL engage with the partner country to address any recommendations in DOL's report and to attempt to find a mutually agreeable solution to any potential violation of FTA labor provisions.

[51] For information about USTR's and DOL's efforts to monitor Guatemala's and Colombia's implementation of other labor initiatives, see app. III.

[52] GAO-09-439.

[53] Office of the U.S. Trade Representative, "Ambassador Kirk Announces New Initiatives for Trade Enforcement" (press release), July 16, 2009, accessed July 18, 2013, http://www.ustr.gov/about-us/press-office/speeches/transcripts/2009/july/ambassador-kirk-announces-new-initiatives-trade.

[54] See GAO, *International Trade: Strategy Needed to Better Monitor and Enforce Trade Agreements*, GAO/NSIAD-00-76 (Washington, D.C.: March 2000).

[55] GAO/NSIAD-00-76. To identify these five steps, we reviewed agency records and interviewed agency officials and staff at several U.S. agencies.

[56] GAO-09-439.

[57] For information about other steps that DOL took in response to our 2009 report's recommendations, see http://gao.gov/products/GAO-09-439.

[58] App. III also discusses the agencies' efforts to monitor implementation of the CAFTA-DR White Paper and the Guatemala Enforcement Plan.

[59] See fig. 1 for information about U.S. agencies' cooperative project funding by FTA partner. In comments on a draft of this report, USTR indicated that 12 of the 20 FTA partners have received, or are expected to receive, some technical assistance from State or Labor.

[60] USTR divided the existing TPSC Subcommittee on Labor to form the Subcommittee on Labor Monitoring and Enforcement and the Subcommittee on Labor Policy and Negotiations.

[61] In addition, according to USTR, the subcommittee is responsible for satisfying public reporting requirements and making eligibility determinations tied specifically to labor standards, such as those in specific preference programs. According to USTR, other TPSC subcommittees may also address enforcement of labor provisions.

[62] USTR staff noted that they also receive information about labor conditions in partner countries from the subcommittee as well as by other means, such as direct coordination with DOL and State staff, discussions with stakeholders such as unions and advocacy groups, communication with FTA partner government officials, and reviews of State cables and reports and news articles.

[63] According to DOL, the labor affairs councils for the Singapore and Australia FTAs have not met since the FTAs went into effect (in 2004 and 2005, respectively). The labor subcommittee (which serves the same purpose as a labor affairs council) for the Jordan FTA has met twice since the FTA took effect, and the labor affairs councils under the remaining FTAs have each met once. The last labor affairs council meeting under CAFTA was in 2008. According to DOL staff, meetings of the labor affairs councils under the Morocco and Peru FTAs have been planned. The labor chapters of the Israel FTA and NAFTA did not provide for labor affairs councils.

[64] According to DOL staff, DOL has been monitoring compliance with FTA labor provisions since NAFTA entered into force in 1994. Before DOL established the Monitoring and Enforcement of Trade Agreements Division, the Trade Agreement Administration and Technical Cooperation Division, in the Bureau of International Labor Affairs' Office of Trade and Labor Affairs, oversaw administration of FTA labor provisions.

[65] According to DOL, the Monitoring and Enforcement of Trade Agreements Division also monitors implementation of FTA labor provisions and other labor conditions through phone calls, e-mails, and interactions with numerous stakeholders, as well as through periodic visits to partner countries, as resources allow.

[66] The five FTA labor submissions exclude any submissions that DOL has received under the North American Agreement on Labor Cooperation.

[67] These eight practices are as follows: (1) define and articulate a common outcome; (2) establish mutually reinforcing or joint strategies; (3) identify and address needs by leveraging resources; (4) agree on roles and responsibilities; (5) establish compatible policies, procedures, and other means to operate across agency boundaries; (6) develop mechanisms to monitor, evaluate, and report on results; (7) reinforce agency accountability for collaborative efforts through agency plans and reports; and (8) reinforce individual accountability for collaborative efforts through performance management systems. GAO, *Results-Oriented Government: Practices That Can Help Enhance and Sustain Collaboration among Federal Agencies*, GAO-06-15 (Washington, D.C.: October 2005). An updated version of this guidance is available at http://www.gao.gov/key_issues/leading_practices_collaboration/issue_summary.

[68] GAO-AIMD-00-21.3.1.

[69] In January 2012, DOL accepted a labor submission for Mexico under the North American Agreement on Labor Cooperation.

[70] DRL also includes a position of Special Representative for International Labor Affairs, which State reported to be vacant during the time of our review.

[71] Section 163 of the Trade Act of 1974, as amended (19 U.S.C. § 2213), requires the President to annually submit to Congress the Trade Policy Agenda and the *Annual Report of the President of the United States on the Trade Agreements Program.* The President delegated this function to USTR in 2004. 69 Fed. Reg. 10133 (Mar. 1, 2004). The President is required to submit a biennial report about labor issues for CAFTA-DR. 19 U.S.C. § 4111(a). This function was delegated to DOL in 2008. 73 Fed. Reg. 38297 (June 30, 2008). State is required to report to Congress annually about human rights in every country worldwide. 22 U.S.C. §§ 2151n and 2304. The Trade Act of 1974 (19 U.S.C. § 2464)

requires the President to submit an annual report to Congress on the status of internationally recognized worker rights within each beneficiary developing country (i.e., countries that benefit from U.S. trade preferences), including the findings of the Secretary of Labor with respect to the beneficiary country's implementation of its international commitments to eliminate the worst forms of child labor. According to DOL, this commitment historically has been fulfilled by State's Human Rights Reports and DOL's Trade and Development Act of 2000 reports on child labor.

[72] 19 U.S.C. § 4111(a).

End Notes for Appendix I

[1] Of the countries we selected for our review, violence against unionists was reported only in Colombia and Guatemala.

[2] ENS and Colombia's Prosecutor General's Office have used different methodologies to determine whether a victim was murdered because of union affiliation. In some cases, ENS has considered a murder union related, while the Prosecutor General's Office has classified the murder as unrelated to union activities. For more information on the differences in data collection methodologies, see Congressional Research Service, *U.S. Colombia Free Trade Agreement: Labor Issues,* RL34759 (Washington, D.C.: January 2012).

[3] We did not determine the cause of the variation, because it was beyond the scope of our work.

[4] A commission of inquiry, the ILO's highest-level investigative procedure, is generally established when a member state is accused of committing persistent and serious violations and has repeatedly refused to address them. According to DOL, as of August 2014, 12 commissions of inquiry had been established.

[5] As a result of a 2006 agreement between the United Nations and the government of Guatemala, CICIG was established as an independent international body designed to support the Guatemalan Public Prosecutor's Office, National Civil Police, and other government institutions in the investigation of crimes committed by members of illegal security forces and clandestine security structures and, in a more general sense, to help disband such groups.

[6] International Labour Organization Governing Body, *Complaint Concerning Non-Observance by Guatemala of the Freedom of Association and Protection of the Right to Organise Convention, 1948 (No. 87), Made by Delegates to the 101st Session (2012) of the International Labour Conference under Article 26 of the ILO Constitution*, GB.320/INS/9 (Mar. 19, 2014).

[7] The Guatemalan Attorney General's Office stated that extinction of criminal liability is defined as an instance in which the government is unable to prosecute as a result of the death of the offender.

[8] International Labour Organization Governing Body, *Complaint Concerning Non-Observance by Guatemala of the Freedom of Association and Protection of the Right to Organise Convention.*

End Notes for Appendix III

[1] Working Group of the Vice Ministers Responsible for Trade and Labor in the Countries of Central America and the Dominican Republic, *The Labor Dimension in Central America and the Dominican Republic: Building on Progress: Strengthening Compliance and Enhancing Capacity* (April 2005), accessed June 7, 2013, http://www.ilo.org/sanjose/lang—es/index.htm.

[2] *Colombian Action Plan Related to Labor Rights* (April 7, 2011), accessed May 29, 2013, http://www.ustr.gov/webfm_send/2787.

[3] These labor initiatives were created outside an FTA framework. Consequently, matters arising from these initiatives would not be addressed through the dispute settlement provisions of an FTA.

[4] *Mutually Agreed Enforcement Action Plan between the Government of the United States and the Government of Guatemala* (2013), accessed August 1, 2013, http://www.dol.gov/ilab/programs/otla/guatemalasub.htm.

[5] According to DOL, its funding for the ILO Verification Project in 2007 and subsequent years totaled $11.6 million. According to ILO staff, the Verification Project represents one of the ILO's most comprehensive evaluation efforts in the region.

End Notes for Appendix IV

[1] DOL has also accepted other labor submissions under the North American Agreement on Labor Cooperation, which we did not examine.

[2] Pursuant to the Bahrain FTA Labor Chapter, parties may only have recourse to dispute settlement under the FTA for matters arising under the commitment to not fail to effectively enforce its labor laws, through a sustained or recurring course of action or inaction, in a manner affecting trade between the parties. Seeking recourse through the dispute settlement chapter of the FTA could lead to the imposition of a monetary assessment or other trade measures. Matters arising under the other commitments in the labor chapter cannot have recourse to dispute settlement under the FTA, but parties are entitled to request consultations on any matter arising under the chapter in an effort to find a mutually agreeable solution. Bahrain FTA, art. 15.6 and ch.19.

In: Protecting Workers' Rights ...
Editor: Samuel T. Stokes

ISBN: 978-1-63483-176-5

Chapter 3

OVERVIEW OF LABOR ENFORCEMENT ISSUES IN FREE TRADE AGREEMENTS*

Mary Jane Bolle

SUMMARY

Since 1993, the Administration has negotiated and Congress has approved 13 free trade agreements (FTAs) that contain labor provisions with different degrees of enforceability. This report identifies two types of labor enforcement issues: (1) those that relate to the FTA provisions themselves, including their definitions and their enforceability, and (2) those that relate to executive branch responsibilities, such as resource availability and determining dispute settlement case priorities. This report does not address other labor issues in the various free trade agreements, including cooperative consultation provisions.

BACKGROUND

The inclusion of enforceable labor provisions—that is, those subject to dispute resolution procedures—in various trade agreement authorities and related reciprocal trade agreements has evolved over time.[1] At first, U.S. trade

---

* This is an edited, reformatted and augmented version of a Congressional Research Service publication RS22823, prepared for Members and Committees of Congress, dated January 29, 2014.

policy focused on lowering tariffs on goods. It was later extended to various types of nontariff barriers.

Labor principles and standards are not subject to World Trade Organization (WTO) rules and disciplines. The International Labor Organization (ILO), an arm of the United Nations founded in 1919, is the multilateral organization with responsibility for labor issues. For nearly 90 years, the ILO has been working to create, through adoption at its annual International Labor Conferences of Member countries, *Conventions*, which set international standards.

The ILO has adopted at least 183 Conventions, 8 of which define 4 "core labor" principles. This occurred when first, a U.N. Social Summit in Copenhagen, Denmark, in 1995 declared that four categories of principles and rights at work are fundamental: (1) freedom of association and collective bargaining; (2) the elimination of forced labor; (3) the elimination of child labor; and (4) the elimination of discrimination in respect of employment and occupation.[2] The ILO then responded by pulling these together as the 1998 *ILO Declaration on Fundamental Principles and Rights at Work and its Follow-Up*. The *Declaration* commits all ILO Member States, whether or not they have ratified the specific conventions, to respect the labor principles in these four key areas. *The Follow-Up*, among other things, calls for reports by developing countries that have not ratified one or more of the core Conventions, on the status of their implementation of the various rights.[3]

The United States had unilaterally promoted the development of "internationally recognized worker rights," principles similar to those in the *ILO Declaration,* through its trade preference laws for developing countries. These trade preference laws cover five main programs: the *Generalized System of Preferences* (GSP), 1975; the *Caribbean Basin Initiative* (CBI), 1983; the *Andean Trade Preference Act* (ATPA), 1991; and the *African Growth and Opportunity Act* (AGOA), 2000; and *the Haiti Opportunity through Partnership Act* (HOPE), 2006. These laws all require that as a condition of obtaining and maintaining program eligibility, beneficiary countries must take steps to afford their workers "*internationally recognized worker rights*." These rights are listed in *Trade Act of 1974,* as amended (Section 507), as similar to ILO core labor principles listed above, except the U.S. list substitutes for the fourth principle listed above: "acceptable conditions of work with respect to minimum wages, hours of work, and occupational safety and health."[4]

In 1996, backed by the United States and other developed countries, the then-124-member WTO debated whether to form a committee to look into the relationship between trade and labor standards. Developing countries, in the majority, argued that the issue had no place in the WTO framework; was little more than a smokescreen for protectionism; and was a bid by industrial nations to undermine the comparative advantage of lower-wage trading partners.[5] Ultimately they prevailed. The Singapore Ministerial Declaration, reporting on what they decided, stated that the ILO (rather than the WTO) would be the "competent body to set and deal with ... internationally recognized core labor standards."[6] The ILO has no enforcement tools, but rather promotes labor standards through consensus, moral suasion, and technical assistance.

Inclusion of labor provisions in bilateral U.S. trade agreements has evolved. The first two U.S. FTAs with Israel, 1985, and Canada, 1988, did not include labor provisions. This pattern began to change after 1993, when a number of factors came into play. First, the United States began to undertake FTA negotiations with lesser-developed countries. Second, it became increasingly accepted that labor issues were related to trade and trade policy. Third, consensus broadened that globalization had both costs and benefits. The benefits tend to be broadly dispersed and include relatively higher economic growth and productivity and greater access to lower-priced goods. The costs tend to be concentrated in import-competing sectors where there may be downward pressure on wages and job displacement. In developing countries, pressures to become a low-cost producer can lead to diminished working conditions and diminished worker rights. Fourth, business groups have increasingly been willing to make some concessions to labor groups in order to promote trade agreements and pave the way for greater trade with and investment in developing countries.

LABOR ENFORCEMENT IN U.S. FREE TRADE AGREEMENTS

Since 1993, the United States has negotiated 13 FTAs that include 19 countries.[7] These are, chronologically, the North American Free Trade Agreement (NAFTA) with Mexico and Canada; bilateral agreements with Jordan, Chile, Singapore, Australia, Morocco, Bahrain, and Oman; a regional agreement known as CAFTA-DR, with the Dominican Republic and the five Central American Countries (Costa Rica, El Salvador, Guatemala, Honduras, and Nicaragua); and bilateral FTAs with Peru, Colombia, Panama, and South

Korea. The last four agreements reflect a bipartisan compromise on labor language as delineated in the "Bipartisan Trade Deal" (popularly known as the "May 10th Agreement,") jointly agreed to between the leadership in Congress and the Administration on May 10, 2007. This agreement calls for, among other things, two additional labor provisions in FTAs: (1) a fully enforceable commitment that FTA countries will adopt, maintain, and enforce in their laws and practice, the basic international labor standards as stated in the 1998 *ILO Declaration;* and (2) the use of identical enforcement provisions for labor and the other provisions in the agreements. Labor and enforcement provisions in these various trade agreements can be categorized into four different models.

Model 1

For *NAFTA*, labor provisions are included in the *North American Agreement on Labor Cooperation (NAALC)*, a side agreement, rather than in the main agreement. Under NAALC, countries agree to enforce their own labor laws and standards. However, under NAALC, the only provision enforceable with sanctions is a Party's "persistent pattern of failure ... to effectively enforce its occupational safety and health, child labor or minimum wage technical standards," where that failure is trade-related and covered by mutually recognized labor laws (Article 29). By comparison, all provisions relating to commercial operations are enforceable under the *NAFTA*. Furthermore, the labor side agreement has different enforcement procedures than does the main agreement, and places limits on monetary enforcement assessments, with suspension of benefits for noncompliance. There are no monetary assessments under the *NAFTA*.

Model 2

In the *U.S.-Jordan Free Trade Agreement*, labor provisions and commercial provisions share the same dispute resolution procedures. Among labor provisions, each Party agrees to "not fail to effectively enforce its labor laws ... in a manner affecting trade" (Article 6.4). Under the *Jordan* agreement, labor laws are defined as U.S. *internationally recognized worker rights.* All labor provisions and commercial provisions are equally enforceable. If the dispute is not resolved under procedures specified, the affected Party shall be entitled to take "any appropriate and commensurate measure" (Article 17.2(b)). However, in an exchange of letters between the USTR Robert Zoellick and Jordanian Ambassador Marwan Muasher before Congress considered the implementing legislation in 2001, the governments reportedly agreed to resolve any potential disputes without resorting to trade sanctions.[8]

Model 3

Seven trade agreements with 12 different countries (Chile, Singapore, Australia, Morocco, Bahrain, Oman, and the six CAFTA-DR countries) include only one enforceable labor provision: each country "shall not fail to effectively enforce its labor laws ... in a manner affecting trade between the Parties." The agreements define *labor laws* as "a Party's statutes or regulations ... that are directly related to" the list of U.S. *internationally recognized worker rights*. All provisions in these agreements relating to commercial operations are enforceable. The seven trade agreements share many of the same procedures for labor and commercial disputes. Procedures for labor disputes place limits on monetary penalties, whereas those for commercial disputes do not. Suspension of benefits is a "last recourse" option for both types of disputes.

Model 4

On May 10, 2007, the bipartisan leadership in Congress and the Administration agreed to a *Bipartisan Trade Deal* to include, among other things, provisions in pending FTAs: with Peru, Colombia, Panama, and South Korea. These are (1) a fully enforceable commitment that Parties to free trade agreements would adopt and maintain in their laws and practices the *ILO Declaration*; (2) a fully enforceable commitment prohibiting FTA countries from lowering their labor standards; (3) new limitations on "prosecutorial" and "enforcement" discretion (i.e., countries cannot defend failure to enforce laws related to the five basic core labor standards on the basis of resource limitations or decisions to prioritize other enforcement issues); and (4) the same dispute settlement mechanisms or penalties available for other FTA obligations (such as commercial interests).[9]

The four concepts were incorporated into all four agreements in virtually identical form. The language appears to limit item (1) in the May 10th

Agreement, described above, by including two footnotes to the key provision: that each Party shall adopt and maintain in its statutes, regulations, and practices, the *rights* as stated in the *ILO Declaration and its Follow-Up*. The first footnote limits obligations of Parties to those specified in the *ILO Declaration* (i.e., without also including the *Follow-Up*). The second footnote requires that a party seeking to challenge violations must demonstrate that the failure to adopt or maintain ILO core labor principles has been "in a manner affecting *either* trade *or* investment between the two countries."[10] In Model 4 resolution of disputes may involve monetary assessments (with no dollar limits) and, if they are not paid, suspension of benefits until the non-conformity is eliminated. The most recent agreements were approved by Congress in the following implementing bills: with Peru, in 2007 (P.L. 110-138); with South Korea in 2011 (P.L. 112-41); with Panama in 2011 (P.L. 112-43); and with Colombia in 2012 (P.L. 112-42).

Enforcement Issues

Based on the differences between labor and commercial FTA provisions articulated in the four models, policy issues can be divided into two categories: the differences in labor vs. commercial provisions themselves (issues 1-3 below); and the differences stemming from the agencies charged with that enforcement (issues 4 and 5 below).

1. Only Some Labor Provisions Are Enforceable

Under Models 2 and 4, all labor provisions in trade agreements are technically enforceable.[11] In Models 1 and 3, only certain labor provisions in trade agreements are enforceable. All commercial provisions in trade agreements are fully enforceable under all models. Under NAFTA, covered by Model 1, the labor side agreement, *NAALC*, as mentioned, includes one enforceable provision: a country must enforce a few of its labor standards—those relating to child labor, minimum wages, and occupational safety and health. A country is not required to enforce its laws relating to the most basic core labor rights—the right to organize and bargain collectively—issues which account for the majority of the labor submissions filed with *NAALC*.[12] The FTAs covered by Model 3 also include only one enforceable labor provision, but it is broader in scope than that in the NAALC: countries must enforce *all* of their own laws relating to *internationally recognized worker rights* in a manner affecting trade between the Parties.

2. Different Enforcement Procedures for and Caps on Penalties for Labor Provisions

Model 1 has separate and dissimilar enforcement procedures for violation of labor as opposed to other provisions. Model 3 has relatively similar procedures for violations under both types of provisions. However, both Models 1 and 3 place caps on potential maximum monetary penalties for violation of labor provisions, but place no caps on penalties for violations of other provisions. Models 2 and 4 have a single set of enforcement procedures covering labor and other provisions and place no caps on penalties. However, as mentioned, under the Model 2, U.S.-Jordan FTA, the Parties agree to make every attempt to arrive at a mutually agreeable resolution through consultations and without application of the FTA's dispute settlement procedures.

3. Limits Placed on Scope of Definition of a Term in Labor Provisions

Labor provisions in Model 4 agreements are "fully enforceable" through the same dispute resolution procedures available for other disputes. However, a footnote limits a key labor provision—that countries adopt and maintain in their laws and practices, the rights as stated in the *ILO Declaration*. The footnote limits the scope of the definition, as mentioned, by saying, "The obligations set out in Article 17.2, as they relate to the ILO, refer only to the *ILO Declaration*." This would suggest that trading Partners could be held to the principles of the *Declaration*, but not the details of the Conventions and not the *Follow-Up* procedures.[13] Some observers have raised concerns that some of the details in some of the ILO core labor standard conventions conflict with some U.S. labor laws, particularly state laws.

4. Differentials in Procedures for Considering Disputes on Labor vs. Other Provisions

Differences in the way that commercial and labor disputes are considered by the Department of Commerce (DOC) and the Department of Labor (DOL) can be summarized as follows: The DOC receives complaints about compliance with trade agreements from the Market Access and Compliance Office's Trade Compliance Center "hotline," industry groups, trade associations, Congress, U.S. Foreign Commercial Service officers, the USTR *National Trade Estimates Report*, and other sources. It uses its many resources to conduct research on compliance cases.[14] The DOL does not have a comparable "hotline," but does have procedures for receiving complaints about labor violations under a free trade agreement.[15] The DOL also states (1) that its core mission is primarily to protect the needs of U.S. workers, rather than those of other countries, which is where complaints about labor conditions related to trade agreements typically arise; and (2) that its international responsibilities include ensuring compliance with labor provisions of trade agreements and trade preference programs. The DOL receives information on foreign labor conditions from a number of sources including trade unions, Congress, Department of State labor officers at U.S. embassies, and the State Department's *Country Reports on Human Rights Practices*. The DOL, like the DOC, may take action to resolve an issue at any stage prior to dispute resolution.[16] Any case not so resolved, may be referred by the respective agency to the Office of the USTR.

5. Priorities for Disputes to be Pursued by the USTR

Labor submissions have been filed with the DOL alleging violations of the labor provisions of the FTAs involving a number of countries, including Guatemala, Bahrain, Honduras, the Dominican Republic, Mexico, and Peru. However, to date, none of these disputes has resulted in formal consultation between the USTR and a foreign government, potentially leading to dispute resolution. Two cases currently pending are: one involving Guatemala, on which negotiations are still proceeding short of formal consultation; and another involving Bahrain, on which the Department of Labor has recommended to the USTR that the United States launch formal consultations.[17]

Should a case not be resolved short of dispute resolution, the USTR must decide which cases it will pursue based on priorities. The USTR is a small operation. Entering into the dispute resolution process is a lengthy, involved, expensive process in terms of both personnel and resources. The USTR typically chooses cases to pursue based on a number of factors. These may include cases that involve clear violations, could clarify particular issues and/or be cases the USTR believes it can win, based on evidence and facts.

End Notes

[1] Trade promotion authority refers to presidential authority to enter into trade agreements that Congress considers under expedited procedures (most recently in Title XXI of the Trade Act of 2002, P.L. 107-210). For more information, see CRS Report RL33743, Trade Promotion Authority (TPA) and the Role of Congress in Trade Policy, by William H. Cooper.

[2] United Nations World Summit for Social Development, Copenhagen. March 6-12. 1995.

[3] ILO Declaration on Fundamental Principles and Rights at Work and its Follow-Up: About the Declaration. From the ILO website, at http://www.ilo.org.

[4] See Trade Act of 1974 (P.L. 93-618 as amended), Sec. 507 (4)(E).

[5] World Trade Organization, Singapore Ministerial Declaration, adopted December 13, 1996, Sec. 4, Core Labour Standards.

[6] See WTO press brief on Trade and Labour Standards, http://www.wto.org/ english/thewto_e/ minist_e/min96_e/labstand.htm.

[7] The U.S.-Israel Free Trade Agreement, which went into effect in 1985, did not contain any labor provisions.

[8] Governments: "would not expect or intend to apply the Agreement's dispute settlement enforcement procedures ... in a manner that results in blocking trade." Jordan Free Trade Agreement Approved by Finance and Ways and Means, Inside U.S. Trade, July 27, 2001.

[9] Text: Congress Administration Trade Deal, Inside U.S. Trade, May 11, 2007; and Trade Facts: Bipartisan Trade Deal. Office of the USTR. Bipartisan Agreement on Trade Policy, May 2007.

[10] Labor chapter of each of the four FTAs, footnote 2.

[11] Under the two-page dispute settlement section in the U.S.-Jordan FTA, which includes much less detail in its procedures than do Model 4 FTAs, if the Joint Committee does not resolve the dispute within 30 days after the presentation of the panel report, the affected Party shall be entitled to take "any appropriate and commensurate measure." However, the dispute settlement, begins with language specifying that "the Parties shall make every attempt to arrive at a mutually agreeable resolution through consultations," and, as mentioned earlier, this provision was reinforced by a mutual exchange of letters between the two countries before Congress considered the implementing legislation.

[12] U.S. Department of Labor, Office of Trade and Labor Affairs.

[13] The United States has ratified only two of the eight ILO core labor principles, although most of their substance is covered by U.S. law.

[14] Phone conversation with Commerce Department officials February 15, 2008.

[15] Procedural guidelines for submitting complaints to the DOL, Office of Trade and Labor Affairs (OTLA) under a labor chapter of a free trade agreement are located in the Federal Register, Vol. 7, p. 245. December. 21, 2006.

[16] Phone conversation with USTR officials, April 4, 2008.

[17] World Trade Online, U.S., Guatemala Takes Another Stab at Resolving CAFTA Labor Fight, December 22, 2011; and DOL Report Recommends Bahrain Consultations Over FTA Labor Violation, January 3, 2013.

INDEX

D

E

F

G

L

M

N

O

P

R

S

T

U

V

W